Erechtheum Papers

Analecta Gorgiana

225

Series Editor
George Kiraz

Analecta Gorgiana is a collection of long essays and short monographs which are consistently cited by modern scholars but previously difficult to find because of their original appearance in obscure publications. Carefully selected by a team of scholars based on their relevance to modern scholarship, these essays can now be fully utilized by scholars and proudly owned by libraries.

Erechtheum Papers

Leicester Holland

gorgias press

2009

Gorgias Press LLC, 180 Centennial Ave., Piscataway, NJ, 08854, USA

www.gorgiaspress.com

Copyright © 2009 by Gorgias Press LLC

Originally published in

All rights reserved under International and Pan-American Copyright Conventions. No part of this publication may be reproduced, stored in a retrieval system or transmitted in any form or by any means, electronic, mechanical, photocopying, recording, scanning or otherwise without the prior written permission of Gorgias Press LLC.

2009

ISBN 978-1-60724-454-7 **ISSN 1935-6854**

Extract from *The American Journal of Archaeology*, vol. 28 (1924).

Printed in the United States of America

American School
of Classical Studies
at Athens

ERECHTHEUM PAPERS
[PLATE I]

FOREWORD

For some years past the American School of Classical Studies at Athens has been making an exhaustive study of the Erechtheum, and many hitherto unobserved details have been noted and new deductions drawn by those concerned in the work. Some of this material has already been published in the AMERICAN JOURNAL OF ARCHAEOLOGY;[1] the rest is shortly to appear in a general publication of the Erechtheum under the editorship of Dr. James M. Paton. In developing the theories contained in the following papers I have been allowed the freest access to all the unpublished material, and I have also gained much profit from suggestions by Messrs. Hill and Caskey and from long discussions with them. I wish, therefore, to acknowledge here my profound indebtedness to the gentlemen concerned, and at the same time to claim indulgence from the reader for statements for which specific references cannot be given until the general work shall have appeared.

Under these circumstances also, it does not seem to me worth while to burden these papers with bibliographies and discussions of the divers theories contained in the considerable mass of writing which the Erechtheum has already provoked. There is more space and more reason for such matter in the exhaustive publication of the School. Here, in an effort for brevity and in the hope of lucidity, I shall confine myself to a simple statement of the evidence found in the building itself and in a few classic literary sources, and to a non-argumentative presentation of my own theories. Footnotes will be reduced to a minimum and references given only when statements in the text are based on the work of others.

I

THE REMAINS OF THE PRE-ERECHTHEUM[2]

Our earliest definite information concerning the fifth century building on the Acropolis at Athens, called the Erechtheum, is con-

[1] *A.J.A.* Vol. X, 1906, O. M. Washburn, August Frickenhaus, 'The Building Inscription of the Erechtheum.'
Vol. X, 1906, G. P. Stevens, 'The East Wall of the Erechtheum.'
Vol. XII, 1908, L. D. Caskey and B. H. Hill, 'The "Metopon" in the Erechtheum.'
Vol. XIV, 1910, B. H. Hill, 'Structural Notes on the Erechtheum.'
Vol. XVII, 1913, W. B. Dinsmoor, 'Attic Building Accounts III, The Erechtheum.'
See also L. D. Caskey, *Ath. Mitt.* 1911, 'Die Baurechnung der Erechtheion fur das Jahr 409–8 v. Chr.'

[2] A great part of the discoveries and deductions set forth in this first paper are due to Mr. B. H. Hill. Specifically, the credit for the discovery of the curious

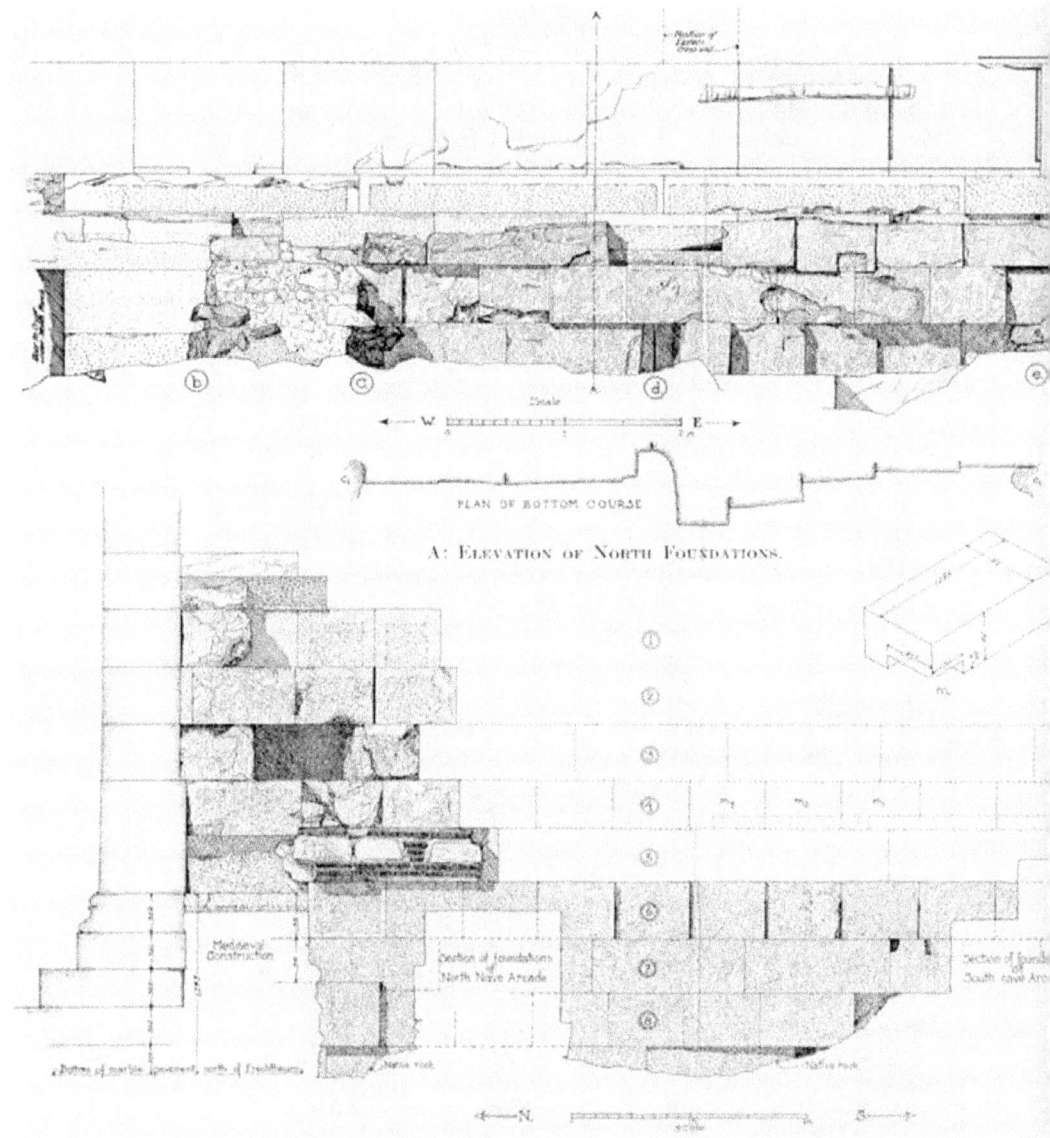

NORTH AND EAST FO

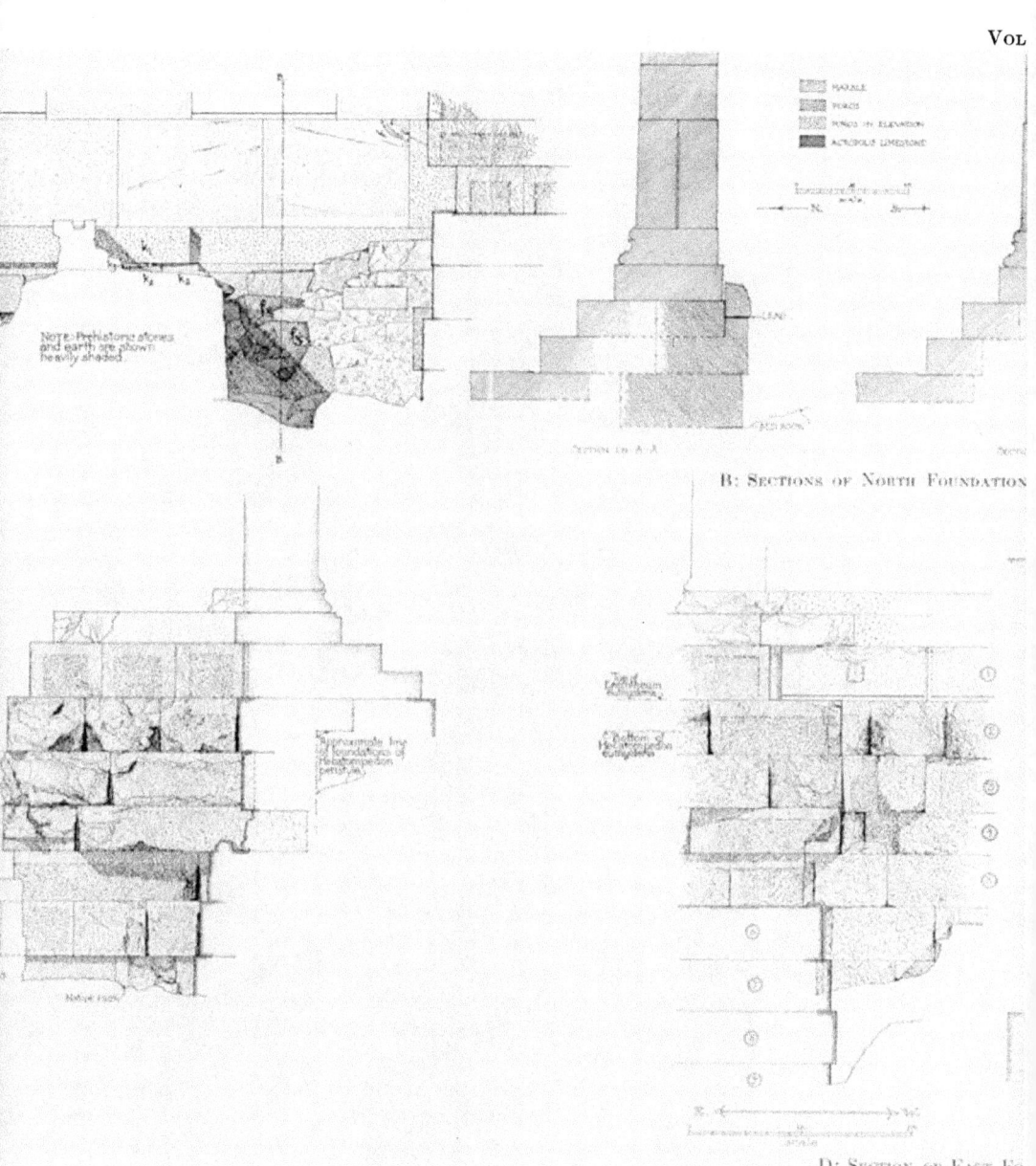

Vol. XXVIII (1924), Plate I

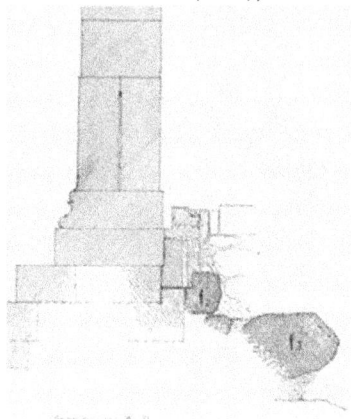

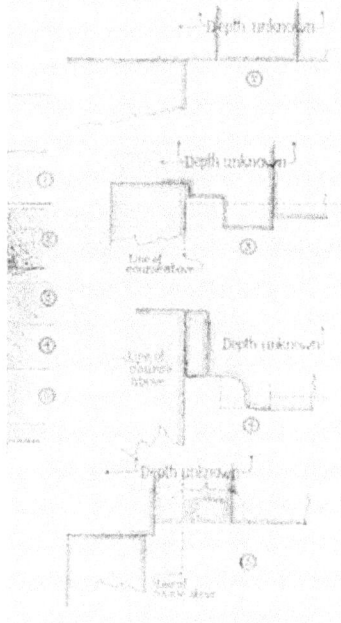

East Foundations.

tained in an inscription dated 409-408 B.C. dealing with its construction. It is very generally believed, however, that the sanctity of the site long antedated the late fifth century edifice, and occasional attempts have been made to reconstruct from pictorial and literary evidence some pre-Erechtheum shrine upon the spot. In support of the theory of the existence of such a structure attention has been called to an area close to the south wall (i, Fig. 1), within the classic building, where the rock of the Acropolis appears to have been roughly leveled.[1] This area, it is suggested, was dressed to form the bed of the southeast corner of a building running diagonally toward

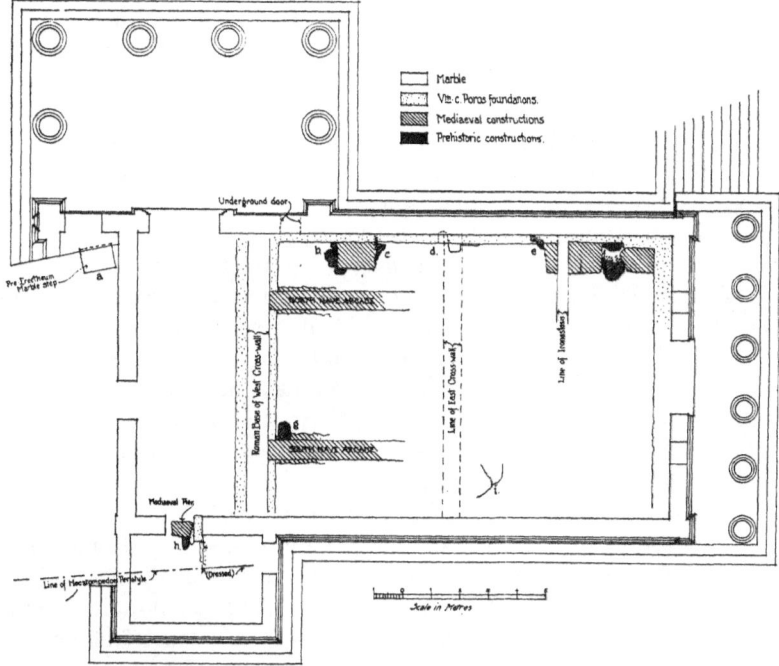

FIGURE 1.—SKETCH PLAN OF ERECHTHEUM.

arrangement beneath the entrance from the North Porch into the Pandroseum, and its explanation; the related explanation of the poros wedges along the inside of the north wall of the Erechtheum; and the observation of the change in the surface of the foundations of the peristyle of the Hecatompedon, belong entirely to him. The significance of the peculiar cuttings in the foundation blocks of the east wall of the Erechtheum and in those of the southeast corner, was first noted by Dr. G. W. Elderkin.

As all these observations are intimately connected with the bases on which I have built my theories concerning the Erechtheum and related areas, Messrs. Hill and Elderkin have generously permitted me to include them with my own material. Needless to say I am deeply grateful. I am indebted to W. B. Dinsmoor for permission to use as PLATE I, A, a measured drawing which he prepared in Athens some years ago.

[1] Heberdey, *Altattische Porosskulptur*, pp. 174 ff., fig. 184. The cuttings are labeled "a" and "b" in his illustration (see below, note 1 on p. 3).

the northwest. Up to the present no other direct material evidence has been adduced in proof of the existence of earlier structures. Yet ample indications of such do exist within the Erechtheum, though they have so far escaped observation.

The nature and form of the older structures indicated is by no means clear, yet since any reconstruction must satisfy the postulates of the evidence, our first concern is to state the facts, and so prepare the way for speculative elaboration.

The bulk of this evidence lies along the inside of the foundations of the north wall. These, at several points, are concealed by adjacent constructions of various periods (PLATE I, A and Fig. 1). The farthest of these to the west is the end of a wall of large poros blocks, the foundations of the western cross wall. This wall originally divided off a wide hall running north and south across the west end of the classic Erechtheum. Later, when the building was converted into a Christian church, this hall served as the narthex, and still later covered a cistern cut in the rock below. Just to the east of the cross wall a small underground door, part of the fifth century construction, gives access to a crypt below the north porch. A metre or so farther east, is a mass of concrete masonry of post-classic date which served as the basis for some indeterminable construction against the north wall. Then, well toward the eastern end of the building, the Christians built the iconostasis of their church, the marble sill of which—borne on a similar mass of concrete masonry—still abuts against the north wall and conceals and preserves, for a little space, remains of pre-classic construction lying inside the fifth century foundations.[1]

The foundations of the fifth century are of poros ashlar, laid normally on beds cut in the rock of the Acropolis; but at one point, where the western face of the foundations under the iconostasis touches the northern wall (e, Fig. 1 and PLATE I, A), the second course of poros ashlar overlaps and rests upon a loose fragment of Acropolis limestone. This has been cut into on its upper surface and dressed with a horizontal and a vertical face to receive the bottom and side of the overlapping block (e_1, Fig. 2). It does not itself rest upon the native rock but on a natural slab of purplish black stone veined with thick layers of white quartz (e_2). It is hardly conceivable that this rough underpinning could have been inserted after the poros was laid, nor is it credible that it was an intentional part of the fifth century construction, in view of the poor

[1] Two other such masses of concrete masonry lie along the north wall, one very low, just east of the line of the classic east cross wall, and one at the extreme east end. Corresponding constructions once existed along the inside of the south wall also, and it is the cutting for one of these that Heberdey has cited as evidence of a pre-Erechtheum (see above, p. 2 and note 3). The two first mentioned in our text, however, are the only ones which preserve pre-classic masonry; they are, therefore, the only ones shown on the sketch plan.

bedding and the very small area of it that would give support. Wherefore it appears that some earlier structure of undressed stone already stood here when the poros blocks were laid, and that for

FIGURE 2.—EARLY CONSTRUCTION AGAINST FOUNDATIONS OF NORTH WALL: CENTRAL SECTION.

some reason the builders of the Erechtheum respected this earlier structure, and instead of removing it merely cut it where necessary to receive their newer work.

At the east side of the iconostasis another stone of similar character has been preserved (f_1, Figs. 3 and 9). This one does not extend under the poros foundations, but its north face seems to have been broken to a plane surface so that the latter might be set against it. Below this again, extending southward to a point 1.50 m. from the inner face of the north wall, are other pieces of Acropolis limestone quite unworked. So far as their own appearance goes they might well belong to the mediaeval construction below the iconostasis, but between and under them there is only clean earth, free from the marble chips and mortar which are characteristic of the adjacent and superposed Christian masonry. Immediately to the east lies another piece of Acropolis stone, larger than any of the preceding (f_2, PLATE I, A and Fig. 3), cut on top and to the north to form a bed for overlapping poros blocks. This stone rests on a similar one, against which to the southeast is an even larger stone (f_3, PLATE I, A and Fig. 3), some 60–75 centimetres in diameter, reaching to a point about 1.50 m. south of the inner face of the north wall. The joints between all of these are quite free from marble chips or mortar; on the east they join a mass of rubble masonry of which the upper part is clearly shown to be post-Erechtheum by the presence of marble fragments and brick and marble chips in the filling between the

FIGURE 3.—EARLY CONSTRUCTION AGAINST FOUNDATIONS OF NORTH WALL: EASTERN SECTION.

stones, while the lower part is just as clearly shown to be neither Roman nor mediaeval because of the complete absence of any scrap of marble.

The pier of post-Erechtheum masonry which has been mentioned as lying further west along the north wall, just east of the underground door, has also preserved a lower stratum of Acropolis stones quite free from marble and mortar, beneath the mass of marble and Acropolis limestone concrete. One of these lower stones on the eastern face of the pier (c_1, Fig. 4) extends for some twenty centimetres into the poros foundations of the north wall. There is no conceivable reason why at any time a hole should have been dug and this stone thrust into the poros structure, so it must be that when the poros was laid the stone was already in place, and being considerably harder than the poros—it is of the black and white stone mentioned before—was not itself dressed down but had the newer work cut to fit around it. On the western side of the pier, however, the foundations of the Erechtheum form the jambs of the underground door and are of marble. Here a piece of Acropolis stone has been clearly cut to receive the juxtaposed marble blocks (b_1, Fig. 5). Other pieces of the same sort form the basis of the pier (c_2, c_3, c_4, c_5,

b_2, b_3, b_4, b_5, etc., Figs. 4 and 5), apparently throughout its whole area. They have been preserved by it at one point to a distance about 1.25 m. south of the inner face of the north wall.

FIGURE 4.—EARLY CONSTRUCTION AGAINST FOUNDATIONS OF NORTH WALL: WESTERN SECTION.

But if mediaeval constructions have preserved *in situ* a small amount of this ancient and unappreciated masonry, the mediaeval constructors, perhaps aided by later archaeologists, have certainly removed a much larger quantity of it. For a series of shallow cuttings of irregular form on the face of the poros foundations of the north wall (PLATE I, A) show where these were trimmed to fit against rough early work that filled the gap from the iconostasis at the east to the line of the eastern cross wall and probably on to the concrete pier at the west; though for this latter part the indications are somewhat less certain. At one point, on the line of the eastern cross wall (d, Fig. 1 and PLATE I, A), the lowest row of poros blocks was cut to fit around a projection that extended into it for a depth of some 35 cm. There is, of course, no way of identifying the uncut Acropolis stones that were taken by later builders from this ancient wall, but in the foundations of a fragment of Christian construction in the southeast corner of the nave of the church, are two pieces which we can be reasonably sure once lay against the north wall, or formed part of some early construction in an analogous position, where fifth century work was fitted against it. For one side of each of them is dressed to a plane surface while the other sides are quite unworked. Such a dressing is not to be accounted for by the normal practice of ancient or mediaeval times.

Further evidence as to the existence, and somewhat as to the nature

FIGURE 5.—FOUNDATIONS BY UNDERGROUND DOOR TO NORTH PORCH.

of the ancient structure against which the foundations of the north wall were built, is given by a very peculiar detail in the construction of the latter. On the inside of the wall the foundations consist of two courses of large poros ashlar (PLATE I, A). Between the marble jamb of the underground door and the east cross wall the blocks of the lower course are laid as stretchers, with the southern face set to an approximately uniform line. But east of the eastern cross wall they are laid as headers with the ends set to a much more irregular line. Just at the cross wall one of these projects south 35 cm. beyond the general inner line of the foundations to the west, and eastward from this point, each one retreats somewhat further north than its western neighbor (PLATE I, A). The resultant offsets are, however, not of uniform size. The upper course consists throughout of headers, set to an even face in the central part but breaking back slightly at the west end and again toward the east just before reaching the iconostasis. All this seems to indicate that the north face of the ancient structure which lay east of the east cross wall was not absolutely parallel to the line of the later Erechtheum wall, but ran somewhat more northeasterly, and also that at the bottom it projected farther north than at the top. As a result, just west of the iconostasis the upper course of poros rests on the block of ancient masonry already mentioned, which projects northward beneath it. East of the iconostasis the lower course is entirely concealed by ancient masonry and earth, and even the upper course is hidden by a block of Acropolis limestone set against it.

On the outer face the wall is carried by a moulded base and three steps of marble (PLATE I, B). These do not correspond in height with the courses of ashlar on the inner (south) face of the wall. The bottom of the lowest step is level with the top of the lower inner course, but the bottom of the second step is below the top of the second inner course. The latter has, therefore, been cut down in its northern part to receive the poros backers ranging with the second step. The top step, and above this the moulded course at the base of the wall, are formed of blocks of marble which extend clear through the wall. In building this foundation the two courses of large poros blocks were not set to an even southern face, but as has

FIGURE 6.—GENERAL VIEW OF FOUNDATIONS OF NORTH WALL, FROM WITHIN.

been shown, were placed so as to form a reasonable contact with preëxisting rubble work which had itself been trimmed in some places to receive them. The inner (south) face of the upper course, therefore, extends roughly 20 cm. south of the inner face of the marble top step and the wall above. Running along the shelf so formed is a row of curiously cut poros blocks set on edge (Fig. 6). These range from 0.55 m. to 1.55 m. in length, from 0.35 m. to 0.45 m. in height and from 0.15 m. to 0.25 m. in thickness. The inner (south) faces are dressed more or less roughly. The tops are carefully cut in a series of long, irregular, very shallow curves which seem to run from approximately the middle of one block to that of the next. Their length varies from about 0.80 m. to about 1.15 m. and the depth of their concavity from 2 cm. to 5 cm.; all these curved surfaces slope slightly toward the inner (south) face of the blocks. The ends are dressed to form nearly vertical joints, but are cut on a slight diagonal so that there shall be contact between one stone and the next at the outer edge only. The outer (north) faces were roughly dressed before setting and again cut into, in places, to permit the marble blocks outside to be fitted close against them. The most curious thing about these blocks is the presence of lead beneath them and in many of the vertical joints, evidently run in, in a molten condition, from the outer (north) side.

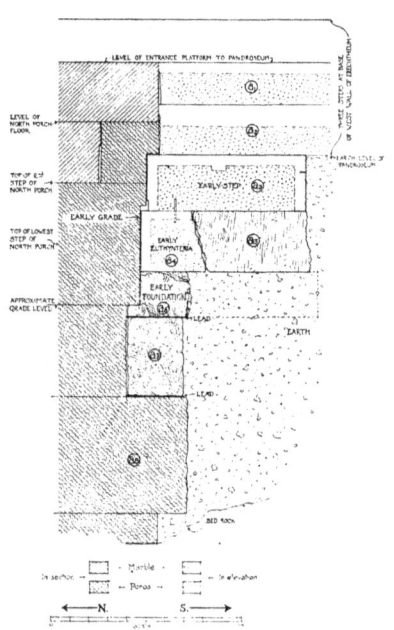

FIGURE 7.—CONSTRUCTION AT ENTRANCE TO PANDROSEUM FROM NORTH PORCH, LOOKING NORTHEAST.

FIGURE 8.—SECTION THROUGH CONSTRUCTION AT ENTRANCE TO PANDROSEUM FROM NORTH PORCH.

Fortunately for the interpretation of all these peculiarities another bit of similar construction has been preserved near by, so completely as to be perfectly intelligible. This occurs in the reëntrant corner formed by the outside of the west wall of the Erechtheum and the westward extension of the north porch (a, Fig. 1). Here the builders of the Erechtheum provided an entrance to the adjacent enclosure of the Pandroseum, at a point where evidently an entrance had already existed (Figs. 7 and 8). For beneath the marble slabs of the late fifth century entrance platform (a_1 and a_2) there are remains of a marble step (a_3) set on a marble euthynteria (a_4), which are certainly of earlier date. Apart from the underpinning built when the modern excavations removed the earth below, this euthynteria is supported only by a small block of poros bedded in lead (a_6). This rests, in turn, upon a larger block of poros set on edge (a_7) and also bedded in lead, which is carried at its eastern end merely by earth and at its western end by one of the great poros blocks (a_8) which form the foundations of the North Porch. To understand the reason for this arrangement it is only necessary to visualize the situation existing when the North Porch was built. When work began the older marble step lay here upon its euthynteria with probably no further foundation than a single course of poros and the earth below. Since the step was of no great weight and the ground level to the north came nearly to the top of the euthynteria, the foundation, though slight, was adequate. But when, in order to lay the adjacent foundations of the North Porch on bed rock, the earth to the north was removed to a depth of a metre below the bottom of the poros course under the euthynteria, the stability of the entire structure was seriously compromised. And since this early step was to serve as support for the new marble platform it was necessary to render it secure. So, the earth having been carefully cut away, one of the large blocks of the foundations of the North Porch (a_8) was laid on bed rock in such a way as to extend slightly under the euthynteria. On this a block on edge (a_7) was pushed in from the north, flat against the unexcavated earth, so that its upper surface came snugly under the bottom of the poros foundation for the euthynteria (a_6). Then molten lead was run into the joints above and below, which, expanding as it cooled, insured that the upper weight should be solidly borne by the lower blocks.

By analogy it becomes evident that the row of curiously shaped poros pieces along the inside of the north wall of the Erechtheum (PLATE I, A and Fig. 6) also served as wedges to transfer the weight of some preëxisting structure above them to the new poros foundations below them. Their tops were carefully shaped to fit the under surface of what they were to carry, their ends and tops were both cut to a slight wedge-like angle so that they could be pushed firmly home from the outside, and lead was run in below them and above—as shown by that which flowed down into the vertical joints between them—to guarantee complete solidity.

But if it is clear that the function of the poros pieces was to support something which projected northward from the ancient rubble wall against which they were placed, it is by no means clear what that something was. The shape of the tops of the poros pieces would indicate that the blocks they supported were neither squarely dressed stones nor rough pieces of Acropolis rock, but apparently something like slabs of naturally cleft stone which without dressing had a very nearly flat surface. The fact that the fifth century floor level in the western half of the building must have come at the bottom of the orthostates, at a level varying from 40 cm. to a possible maximum of only 50 cm. above the tops of the poros pieces, strengthens the conviction that these supported slabs, though this does not hold, of course, for the eastern half of the building, where there is no indication of a floor at this level. On the other hand it is difficult to see why slabs resting on a wall which must have been at least 1.50 m. wide should require such elaborate support for a projection of merely 20 cm. beyond its face. And furthermore, just to the east of the iconostasis (Fig. 9 and PLATE I, A), a projection inwards of one of the marble blocks of the north wall (k_1) has preserved between it and the poros wedge (k_2), here very close below, some broken pieces still *in situ* of what the latter bore, and it is poros (k_3)! Beneath it there is a thin layer of lead, confirming the supposition that lead was run in above as well as below the wedge blocks. Why poros work should show so peculiar a profile on its under surface, and whether we must infer poros slabs in the western section are questions beyond the scope of this first paper, which aims merely to present the material evidence for, and existing remains of older structures on the site of the Erechtheum.

A little light may be thrown, however, by an attempt to date the pre-Erechtheum construc-

FIGURE 9.—FOUNDATIONS AT NORTH END OF ICONOSTASIS.

tions so far examined. The older step and euthynteria beneath the entrance platform from the North Porch are clearly shown by their workmanship and by existent double T clamps, to be of the fifth century. The inner (south) face of the euthynteria had been broken (Fig. 7), apparently before the block was set,[1] which implies that it is a re-used block. The whole seems to be pre-Periclean and post-Persian; it probably dates from a comparatively cheap and rapid restoration of the sanctuaries of the Acropolis soon after the Persians had been driven from the land. But the rubble wall of Acropolis limestone within the building cannot be of the same period, since such construction was not employed at that time. If the evidence did not show clearly that the Erechtheum was built against it, and if the joints were not wholly free from marble chips and mortar, it might well be considered mediaeval, as no doubt it has been considered up to now; but this possibility being barred, the only alternative date for such a wall is one prior to the use of polygonal masonry. In other words it cannot well be later than the eighth century B.C., and may be considerably earlier. In the earth between the stones many fragments of Late Helladic III[2] pottery have been found, but none of any later date. This is not in itself sure proof, but it certainly is a strong indication that the ancient structure inside the Erechtheum was roughly contemporary with the "Cyclopean" fortifications just outside to the northeast, and the "Palace" just to the south. In general the Late Helladic masonry of the Acropolis is built of undressed pieces of Acropolis limestone, but in places the black and white striped stone is also used, and there are occasional long pieces of a coarse grey and white marble which splits naturally into slabs such as seem to be indicated for the top of the ancient wall inside the Erechtheum. On the other hand poros, though it does occur in prehistoric work, as in the column bases south of the Erechtheum, is extremely rare. So it may be that the fragment of poros preserved from the pre-Erechtheum structure is contemporary with that of the mid-fifth century by the North Porch, and at that time may have replaced still earlier Late Helladic slabs.

The original length of the ancient wall cannot be known. At the east it ran up to the foundations of the east wall of the Erechtheum, and since the excavations on the Acropolis in 1886[3] showed no "Cyclopean" remains continuing its line outside the building, it may never have gone any farther in that direction. At the west

---

[1] In order to give support throughout the width of the step, the marble block is backed with one of poros (a_5, Figs. 9 and 10) roughly dressed to fit the broken face of the former.

[2] For this chronological classification, see Blegen, *Korakou*, pp. 120 ff.; *B.S.A.* XXII, pp. 186 f.

[3] Cavvadias and Kawerau, *Ausgrabung der Akropolis*, pl. Γ.

the traces stop one metre before reaching the little underground doorway. It may be that the door stands where a break occurred in the older wall, or the older wall may have been cut when the door was built, or may never have gone any farther west. Just beyond the door come the foundations of the west cross wall of the classic building, and beyond that all evidence for or against the western prolongation of the ancient wall has been thoroughly removed by the construction of the mediaeval cistern. The foundations of the exterior west wall of the Erechtheum do not, however, quite reach to those of the north wall at the northwest corner, and on the inner side are cut and laid in an irregular manner as if affected by some pre-existent construction. This may indicate that the ancient wall continued to this point; on the other hand, since the foundations are treated in a similar way on the outside, where there are actual remains of rough Acropolis limestone masonry, it may quite as well be that some other prehistoric construction stood here at the corner of the Pandroseum, which affected both the outside and inside of the classic west wall foundations, but yet had no direct connection with the long prehistoric wall to the east.

Two other bits of "Cyclopean" stone work exist *in situ* inside the Erechtheum. The sill (h_1, Fig. 10) of the door from which stairs lead up to the Porch of the Maidens (h, Fig. 1) is, at the present time, supported at a height of 1.30 m. above bed rock by a modern pier of poros (h_2, Fig. 10) and by a pier of mediaeval masonry (h_3)

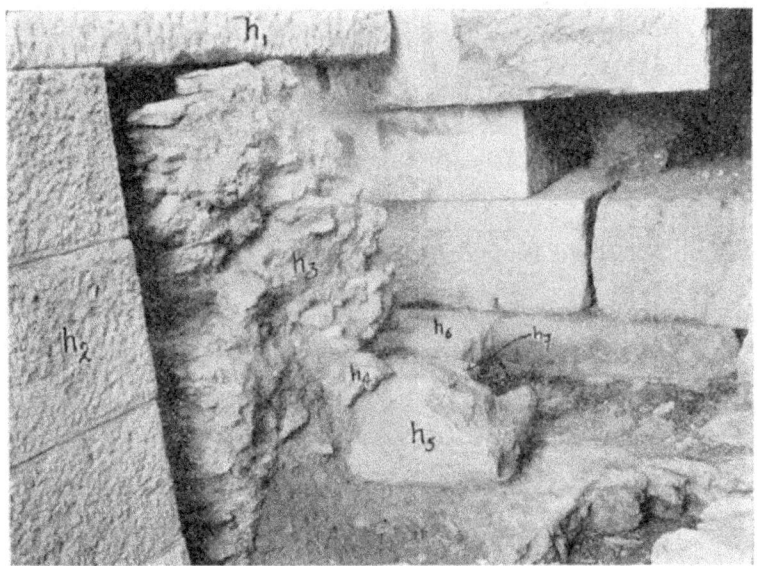

FIGURE 10.—CONSTRUCTIONS BELOW DOOR FROM ERECHTHEUM TO PORCH OF MAIDENS, LOOKING NORTHEAST.

which remains from a mediaeval wall that until 1906 ran under the full length of the sill. Probably the mediaeval support was built at the time the cistern was cut. It is not likely that foundations of classic ashlar stood here at that time and were removed merely to be replaced with a wall of marble and brick fragments set in mortar; moreover, the native rock below shows no sign of cuttings such as were customary for bedding classic foundations. But it is altogether improbable that the heavy sill and the corner of wall to the west which rests upon it, would have been originally laid merely on earth. Therefore, logic compels us to infer here a pre-classic substructure of uncut and unbedded masonry to support the classic sill. And just at the bottom of the south side of the mediaeval pier a few stones of such masonry do actually persist (h_4, h_5). Between them and about them is a little clean earth unmixed with marble chips, while directly upon and enclosing this comes the mediaeval work; the line between the older earth and the later mortar is quite distinct. Further proof of the antiquity of these uncut stones is given by the relation between them and the foundations of the Erechtheum (Figs. 10 and 11). The lowest block beneath the east jamb of the door to the Porch of the Maidens is a large piece of dressed poros 0.63 m. by 0.88 m. by 0.46 m. thick, laid on a carefully dressed bed cut in the native rock (h_6). Its western face is about 0.14 m. away from the eastern face of the lowest piece of Acropolis limestone at the bottom of the mediaeval pier (h_5). The latter piece is laid directly on the native rock without any dressed bed. Its upper surface is approximately level with that of the poros foundation block. Between the two is wedged a small piece of poros (h_7) roughly dressed to fit the space. The arrangement indicates clearly that the piece of Acropolis limestone was already in place when the large poros foundation block was laid, and that the poros wedge was then put in to fill the gap. There is no other explanation for so obviously fitted a wedge.

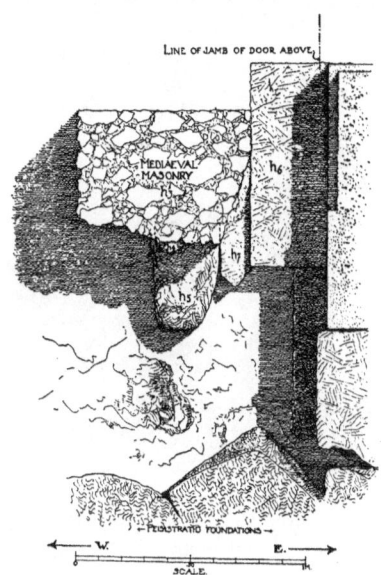

FIGURE 11.—PLAN OF CONSTRUCTIONS BELOW STEPS IN PORCH OF MAIDENS.

The existence of some ancient structure below the stairs in the Porch of the Maidens is further indicated by a hitherto unremarked peculiarity[1] in the treatment of the north face of the foundation wall of the peristyle of the Hecatompedon (Fig. 12). This wall is built of great blocks of Kara stone dressed on their upper and lower surfaces to form horizontal beds, but in plan roughly polygonal. Across the western end of the Hecatompedon the outer face of the foundation wall is entirely rough, showing that originally it was concealed underground. And for the same reason, because of its unfinished surface, the north wall must also have been hidden by a terrace or some other structure or structures reaching from the western end to a point in line with the eastern jamb of the door to the Porch of the Maidens and the eastern edge of the stairway there. From here eastward the wall, above the lowest course, is dressed to an even face. The fact that the vertical joints are more carefully fitted than in the western part indicates that the dressing dates from the erection of the peristyle by the Pisistratids and the fact that the dressing does not stop in any continuous vertical line, but is in each course coterminous with one of the stones in the course, indicates that the stones were dressed before being laid. Obviously then, the change in surface marks the eastern limit of some preëxisting construction extending to the west, behind and close against which at this point, the foundations for the peristyle were laid. The pieces of Acropolis limestone below the sill are probably remains of this earlier construction. It is impossible to say how far eastward the Hecatompedon wall continues to be dressed, for the foundations of the Erechtheum are laid so close to it that one can see into the space between for a distance of only some two and a half metres, but so far at least it shows the same smooth face.

FIGURE 12.—FOUNDATIONS OF PERISTYLE OF HECATOMPEDON, LOOKING EAST UNDER PORCH OF MAIDENS.

[1] Heberdey, *Altaltische Porosskulptur*, fig. 186, suggests in plan that the foundations of the peristyle of the Hecatompedon are dressed to the east of the steps in the Porch of the Maidens. He does not mention this peculiarity in his text, but, perhaps, intends to discuss it in his study of the grave of Cecrops, which is promised in note 1, p. 177.

One of the very puzzling problems of the Erechtheum can now be easily explained by analogy with the sill of the door to the Porch of the Maidens. There is strong evidence on both the north and south walls of the Erechtheum that a wall .65 m. wide crossed it from north to south at a point 7.50 m. west of the east façade. But in the rock of the Acropolis below there is no trace of cuttings such as one would expect for foundations of a fifth century wall, with the possible exception of the bit of level surface advanced by Heberdey as evidence for his pre-Erechtheum.[1] This, however, is somewhat east of the line indicated for the transverse wall. It has, therefore, been maintained that no real wall ever existed at this point.[2] But the discrepancies of the evidence are easily reconciled by the discovery that the sill of the door to the Porch of the Maidens was carried on prehistoric instead of on classic foundations. For a "Cyclopean" wall of rough Acropolis stones requires no cuttings in the rock below, and if removed by later builders or investigators leaves no trace at all. On such a foundation, reverently preserved, the builders of the Erechtheum could and doubtless did erect the east cross wall as part of their new fifth century building.

The last fragment of what may be prehistoric masonry is a single piece of the grey schist-like marble, 0.45 m. wide and 0.09 m. thick, which projects to the north from beneath the mediaeval foundations of the south nave arcade (g, Fig. 1), just to the east of the west cross wall. The length is indeterminable since the stone is in part under the mediaeval wall, but the fact that it lies at right angles to that wall and projects to the north of it suggests that when the wall was built it was already in its present position. Moreover, the mediaeval foundations are laid in mortar on the native rock, while beneath this stone there is only clean earth free from marble, brick, or mortar. It, too, may therefore be part of some Mycenaean construction, perhaps a wall running north and south just to the east of the classic west cross wall.

Beside the indications of prehistoric constructions within the Erechtheum there is clear evidence that work of a later period also stood there and was respected by the late fifth century builders. This evidence is to be found on the inner (west) face of the foundations of the eastern wall and portico (PLATE I, C and D). The floor level of this portico is nearly three metres higher than the floor in the western part of the building, and consequently it requires from seven to nine courses of poros to reach from bed rock to this upper level. Originally the foundations formed a solid mass beneath the whole extent of the portico and east wall, but at some Christian period the central part of this mass was torn out, down to the sixth

---

[1] See above, p. 2 and note 1, and note 1, p. 3.
[2] Elderkin, *Problems in Periclean Buildings*, pp. 38 ff.

poros course (counting down from the portico floor) in order to permit the construction of a proper churchly apse. The poros blocks thus removed were used to form the foundations of the north and south nave arcades. The lowest course in the east wall (No. 9, counting from above) is a stretcher course (PLATE I, C); the blocks of it and the native rock are cut to fit each other. Course 8 is a course of headers of even size, except where it meets the slope of the native rock at the south end and where for some uncertain reason there is an irregularity at the north end.

Course 7 is one of regular stretcher blocks with a single short block at the south end to fill the gap between the southernmost stretcher and the south wall. Such an arrangement implies that the south wall was laid before the eastern one and that the latter was laid, contrary to what one would expect, from north to south. This last block laid is roughly cut into on its west face, apparently to fit an irregularity in the native rock. Both this block and the first stretcher (counting from the south) are set slightly further east than the other blocks of the course. The second stretcher from the south shows two curious cuttings. The upper northern corner is neatly cut away on a concave line, forming a channel which extends into the wall for a depth of 44 cm. This channel apparently has no connection or outlet at its inner end, nor, as the block is probably about 65 cm. thick, does it go clear through this. The cutting affects neither the adjacent block to the north nor the one above, and, therefore, was probably made before laying the block in which it is cut. The only apparent explanations are that the block is a re-used one, though it does not appear so, and that the cutting had some function in its former situation; or that when the block was being prepared or set, this corner proved faulty or was damaged and was cut away simply to even it up. This, though it seems a reasonable enough thing to do, is not a normal Greek practice. Farther south on the same block is another cutting approximately rectangular, 33 cm. wide by 14 cm. down from the top of the block, cut roughly in to a depth of 6 cm.; that is, just to the face of the block in the course above. This last circumstance suggests that the cutting was made after the block above was laid, in which case it is probably not fifth century work, but dates from some Christian construction.

Course 6, always counting from above, is a header course, laid like those below with reasonable regularity. Here again a small block at the southern end indicates that the corresponding course in the south wall was laid before this eastern course. And again at the northern end there is an irregularity in the coursing from which as a starting point the blocks must have been laid toward the south. The central header of this course (seventh from the south) has its eastern face roughly dressed back for a depth of 10 cm. over a width of 40 cm. from the northern edge. This cutting affects neither the block below nor that adjacent, and was, therefore, probably made before or at the time the block was set. I have no explanation to suggest for it.[1] All three of these courses (8, 7, 6) are of approximately the same height—46 to 48 cm.—and all have the western face similarly dressed to a rather smooth picked surface without any anathyrosis, but on several of the blocks of Course 6 there is a slight tooling back like a very shallow drafting around the edge. Each course is set slightly back from the course below so that the face of the wall retreats slightly toward the east as it ascends (PLATE I, D).

The central part of Course 5 has been removed (PLATE I, C); at the north and south ends it consists of stretchers. The length of the southern one is 1.652 m., and three more 1.687 m. long would just reach to the northern one. It seems probable that such was the arrangement, since stretchers 1.30 m. long (four Attic feet, approximately the length of those in Courses 3 and 7, and twice the width of the standard headers) would not fill out the gap evenly. The height of this course varies between 0.455 m. and 0.458 m., *i.e.* it is approximately the same as in the lower courses. It is set back some 19 cm. to the east of the course below; none of the lower courses are set back more than half this distance. Another difference is that the western faces of this show distinct anathyroses. At the southern end the corner is filled by a block which does not align with the faces of either the south or east walls (PLATE I, D, 5). Here again it is probable that the east wall was laid from a point at the north, where again there is an irregularity in the coursing. The cavity formed by the eastward setback of this course was filled up in the Middle Ages, at the northern end at least, by a mass of brick, marble and mortar. A metre and a half of this construction is still in place.

Except for the northernmost block, Course 4 is markedly lower than the other courses, its height being only 0.416 m. to 0.42 m., while the next lowest is the one below, 0.455 m. in height. As the top of this course does not agree with that of the corresponding course in the south wall, but does line up exactly with the top of the orthostates in the north wall, it is possible that the latter determined its height. Only five stones of this course are *in situ* (PLATE I, C), three at the north end and two at the south; they all overhang the course below; their faces being about 30 cm. west of those of Course 5. The northernmost block is of irregular width as well as height, like those below it was apparently used as a gap filler. The next two are perfectly regular headers with joints very nearly cor-

[1] See below, note 1, p. 20.

responding to those two courses below, but in this course as in the fifth, the western faces are cut with anathyroses. Eight headers of the same width filled the space to the remaining southern blocks. The northern one of the latter, though a header of standard width, differs from the northern blocks in that the under side of the part projecting over the course below has been squarely cut back for a height of 11 cm. and a depth of 30 cm. The vertical face at the back of this cutting, which is directly over that of the block below, has an anathyrosis along its southern edge. The block at the extreme south of the course is an unusually long stretcher. Its south end extends so far into the south wall that its exact length cannot be determined (PLATE I, D, 4), but careful probing indicates that it runs back to a point which corresponds very nearly to the line given by the eastward prolongation of the foundations of the peristyle of the Hecatompedon. It is probable, though not absolutely certain, that this long stretcher was the first stone in the course to be laid, but it is certain that it was laid before the easternmost block in the south wall—a small and very soft piece of poros—was dropped into place to fill up the gap between the long stone in the east wall and the last stretcher of the south wall.

Five of the missing eight headers of Course 4 lie now in the foundations of the north nave arcade, and one in those of the south. They can be identified with certainty[1] because of the peculiar height of the course. The remaining two blocks have not been found. The block in the south nave arcade and two of those in the north are like the two headers *in situ* at the north end of Course 4. They are 1.24 m. to 1.28 m. long by 0.64 m. to 0.66 m. wide by 0.412 to 0.417 m. high, that is, in terms of Attic feet of 0.327 m., four feet long by two feet wide. The height was probably originally one and a half feet, and was dressed down seven or eight centimetres after the blocks were laid in order to bring them to a level with the top of the orthostates in the north wall. Two more of the blocks in the north nave arcade are like the headers still *in situ* at the south of Course 4, they are of the same general dimensions as the other headers but have the ends cut back on the under side for a height of 0.122 m. and 0.12 m. and a distance of 0.295 and 0.315 m. respectively. The last of the displaced blocks is unique (m, PLATE I, C); its overall dimensions are normal, 1.248 m. by 0.66 m. by 0.42 m., and it has a cutting on the under side of the end 0.125 m. by 0.30 m., but this cutting instead of running all the way across the block extends only 0.435 m., thus leaving the part to the north, as the block lay in place, uncut for a width of 0.225 m. Obviously this block formed the transition from the cut blocks at the south to the uncut

---

[1] The identification of these blocks is due to Dr. Elderkin, who first called attention to their significance while on a brief visit to Athens in the spring of 1923.

ones at the north, but its exact location is uncertain, since two of the blocks in the course are missing.[1] If these two were uncut headers it must have lain at m_1 (PLATE I, C), if one was cut and one uncut, at m_2, and if both were cut, at m_3. The height of the cutting on the under side of m. is 0.125 m., that on the header in situ is only 0.11 m. We should expect the cuttings on the intermediate blocks to increase in height from south to north. The other two known headers are cut to depths of 0.122 m. and 0.12 m. If these be placed in that order next to m. and two blocks with cuttings 0.116 m. and 0.113 m. assumed next to them, the series will then pass by even gradations of three millimetres per block from south to north. If we were dealing not with poros but with marble, the customary accuracy of workmanship in that material would allow us to place m at m_3 with practical certainty; with the softer, rougher material certainty is gone, but a fairly good presumption persists in favor of that location.

The three courses which come above present no features of especial interest; all three align with the courses of the north and south walls where they meet them, though a little to the west of the corner the south wall is somewhat irregular. Course 3 was presumably made of normal stretchers, four Attic feet long, changing to headers for the three northern blocks. It was certainly laid before the eastern block of the south wall and almost certainly the stretchers were laid from north to south. Course 2 is of normal headers, two Attic feet wide with the exception of the northernmost; it was laid after the corresponding course in the south wall and in this case from south to north. The inner (western) faces of both these courses are in fairly accurate vertical alignment above that of Course 4 (PLATE I, D). Course 1 is made of headers of irregular widths, and as it is set well back (east) from the courses below and corresponds with the two lower steps of the building, it more properly belongs with the superstructure than with the foundations.[2]

A comparison of the peculiarities of this wall with those under the door from the North Porch to the Pandroseum indicates that in the two places the builders were dealing with analogous conditions, and that the cut in the lower part of the blocks in Course 4 and the eastward setback of Course 5 were occasioned by some preëxistent structure against which these new foundations were fitted. Moreover, it seems certain that the preëxistent structure here was not of

[1] It is possible that the cutting in the central block in Course 6 (see above, p. 18) may have been made to fit foundations beneath the construction that occasioned the change in the cutting of the blocks two courses above. In that case the transition stone would probably have been at m_2.

[2] The southern section of Course 1 and the superstructure of the Erechtheum are shown in Plate I, C as being 11 cm. further north than they actually are. This error was not discovered until too late to correct the plate, but the parts involved do not enter into this discussion at all.

Mycenaean, but of dressed and fitted masonry, probably similar to that at the entrance to the Pandroseum and very possibly of the same date. It is also to be noticed that the orientation of the late fifth century Erechtheum exactly agrees with that of this earlier classic construction; and (since the undercut blocks of Course 4 were presumably fitted over a step or sill or some similar stone course exposed on its upper surface and along its eastern edge) it is evident that when the earlier construction was new—perhaps shortly after the Persian wars—the earth to the east of the Erechtheum did not come above this level.[1] The grade level to the west of this line is less certain. If, instead of being a sill leading to an enclosure on the same level as the eastern grade, it was one of a flight of steps leading west, which occasioned the cut in the bottom of Course 4, then the floor within the eastern half of the Erechtheum might have been considerably higher or lower than the grade to the east, depending on whether the steps led up or down.

A section through the foundations of the east wall (PLATE I, D) of the Erechtheum indicates, however, that the earlier construction against which Courses 4 and 5 were built probably went no lower down than the bottom of Course 5. For Courses 6, 7 and 8 project each one a little westward of the one above, which, of course, would not have been the case had they been pushed in against a pre-existing ashlar wall; and there is only one cutting, that on the central block of Course 6, such as would be expected on poros blocks set against Mycenaean masonry. Moreover, since the face of Course 5 is 19 cm. east of that of Course 6, the line of ashlar against which Course 5 was placed must needs have overhung any foundation by at least that amount, though in normal fifth century work the foundation regularly projects somewhat beyond the superstructure. So the vanished construction here was probably a very light one, consisting, say, of a course of marble over which the cutting in Course 4 fitted, supported on a course of poros which probably originally projected only a few centimetres east of the marble course and was trimmed back when the abutting course of the foundations of the Erechtheum was laid. The arrangement would be similar to that of the early marble euthynteria and its poros foundation course at the entrance to the Pandroseum. It is an interesting coincidence that the space between the soffit of the cutting in Course 4 of the eastern foundations of the Erechtheum foundations and the bed of Course 5 is 0.563 m., while in the Pandroseum construction the

---

[1] That is, approximately 1.25 m. below the present grade to the east and south of the Erechtheum, and approximately 0.975 m. below the bottom of the euthynteria of the Hecatompedon peristyle. Of course the ancient sill within the Erechtheum might have stood above the ground like a step, anywhere up to 45 cm. in height; in which case the grade level east of the Erechtheum must have been just so much lower.

marble course is 0.315 m. thick and the poros below it 0.24 m., a total of 0.555 m. The marble course above the euthynteria is 0.295 m. high, exactly the height from the top of the cutting in Course 4 to the top of the course itself. If this is more than mere coincidence, it means that the height of Course 4 was not determined by the orthostates in the north wall, but by an older structure, and, in turn, determined the height of the orthostates. But whereas at the entrance to the Pandroseum the old poros course was carefully supported on the newer work, in the east wall of the Erechtheum the upper surface of Course 6 of the foundations was never dressed down smoothly along the western edge, so that the older work could never have come quite down to it. This indicates that the latter structure was not of great weight and that it was not proposed to support new construction upon it.

Did the older structure continue to the north and south beyond the limits of the cuttings in the under side of Course 4? This is uncertain, but seems probable, since Course 5 is set back throughout its length to the line of the cutting in Course 4. The fact that this latter does not run for the full length of the course may be explained by the supposition that where the cutting exists the ancient sill projected forward to form a threshold for a wide entrance; or it may be that marble was used in this threshold section only, and that a continuation to north and south, of poros, was itself dressed back instead of having the new work cut out to fit over it.

There seems to be quite clear indication in the stones at the east end of the south foundations that some sort of parapet or wall stood upon this hypothetical ancient sill. For when the easternmost stone was laid in the course in the south wall which corresponds to Course 5 of the east wall, (PLATE I, D), its upper surface came just to the level of the top of the ancient sill as indicated by the undercutting in Course 4 of the east wall. But when the stones of the next course were laid this upper surface was dressed down 10 cm. to bring it flush with that of the neighboring stones in the east and south walls, except for a small area south of the end of the hypothetical sill, where the original height was left and the stones of the next course were cut to fit around it as they were laid. This arrangement points to the presence of an ancient block of marble (had it been poros the old work would probably have been cut to fit instead of the new), which rested upon the high area in the block in Course 5, and projected across it into the cavity in the foundation stones of the south wall. Unfortunately this cavity (PLATE I, D, 4) is so roughly worked that it gives no clear idea of the dimensions of the block it was cut to fit. In the course above, however (PLATE I, D, 3), the information is much more definite. Here the easternmost stone in the south wall was laid after the last stone in the east wall and was cut to a peculiar shape in order to fit around both this stone and the marble block of the hypothetical ancient wall. The southern face of the cutting comes directly over that in the course below, but its western face, instead of being roughly scooped out as in the lower block, is squared with proper accuracy, to limit the width of the cutting to 0.323 m.; very slightly less than one Attic foot of 0.327 m. If the ancient marble block ran clear to the southern limit of this cutting its height could not have extended above the top of this course, for the face of Course 3, the next above, lies 5 cm. further north. It is quite possible, however, that the block stopped 5 cm. short of this southern limit and extended upwards for an unascertainable distance.

The missing ancient block was evidently an orthostate, probably two to three Attic feet high by four or more long. Another block about two feet long would fill the gap to the line of the foundations of the Hecatompedon peristyle. If these orthostates formed the base of a wall of normal thickness they must have been backed on the inner (western) side with poros or some other soft building material, for when double marble orthostates form the base of a wall it is customary to have the blocks of equal length with coincident vertical joints running through the wall, and here, apparently, there was no marble western backer as far south as the orthostate to which the south foundations were fitted. Since this whole ancient construction seems to have had little or no foundation, however, it is probable that it was not a poros, or brick, or rubble wall with a marble base along its eastern side, but merely a low parapet of upright marble slabs enclosing the *temenos* which later became the eastern cella of the Erechtheum.

To sum up: the evidence shows clearly that at the time the late fifth century Erechtheum was built, there already existed on the site Mycenaean and classic constructions which were respected and the lines of which were paralleled by the later structure. In the case of the classic pre-Erechtheum at least, the orientation was identical with that of the building which replaced it.

LEICESTER B. HOLLAND

PHILADELPHIA,
1923

ERECHTHEUM PAPERS

II

THE STRONG HOUSE OF ERECHTHEUS

[PLATE VII]

IN the golden age, when legendary kings of prehistoric Greece built "beehive" tombs and spacious halls, and the black ships of the Achaeans pillaged Crete and the Aegean coasts and dared the unstable Euxine, Mycenae was the foremost city in the land and the Corinthia and Argolid and fertile Laconian plain were rich with splendid citadels. But when the tide of iron-weaponed northmen came, this very wealth of gold and bronze led them on and on, till the glory of the Peloponnesus went down in wrack and flames. Legends tell that the conquerors came from Doris, and when they could not force the Achaean barrier at the Isthmus, crossed by water from Naupactus and ranging along the south shore of the gulf made straight by Sicyon and Phlius to Mycenae and the Argolid, and southward still into Laconia. A later backwash to the Corinthia pushed north again across the Isthmus and even up to Megara, but there its power died.

Through all these years, a century perhaps, of raids and inroads and barbarian destruction, Athens, either because she lay aside from the Dorian path or because she was too poor a prize to rouse great covetousness, kept safe within the circuit of her heavy walls. Tradition has it that Athens alone of the citadels of Greece preserved the race and culture of her earlier days. It is certain that while the other cities were destroyed her riches grew. Her rôle in the Homeric poems is very slight,[1] and even some of the scant references to her there are held to be additions of a later time inserted by flattering poets. One "bee-hive" tomb stands in the plain at Menidi; there are ample remains to show that Attica was well settled in late Helladic times, but nothing of any striking

[1] In the *Iliad* there are four very brief mentions of the Athenians and their leader Menestheus (II, 549; IV, 328; XIII, 196, 689) and one where Menestheus is mentioned separately (XII, 331). Aside from the item in the Catalogue of the Ships (II, 549 ff.), which is palpably an interpolation in part, if not altogether, the longest reference is (IV, 328), "He found Menestheus the charioteer, the son of Peteos, standing still, and round him were the Athenians, masters of the battle-cry." This is typical; even their mastery of the battle-cry does not seem to have played much part in the fate of Ilium.
In the *Odyssey*, besides the one mentioned below in our text, there are three casual mentions of Athens as a geographical locality (III, 278, 307; XI, 323), but no mention of Athenians.

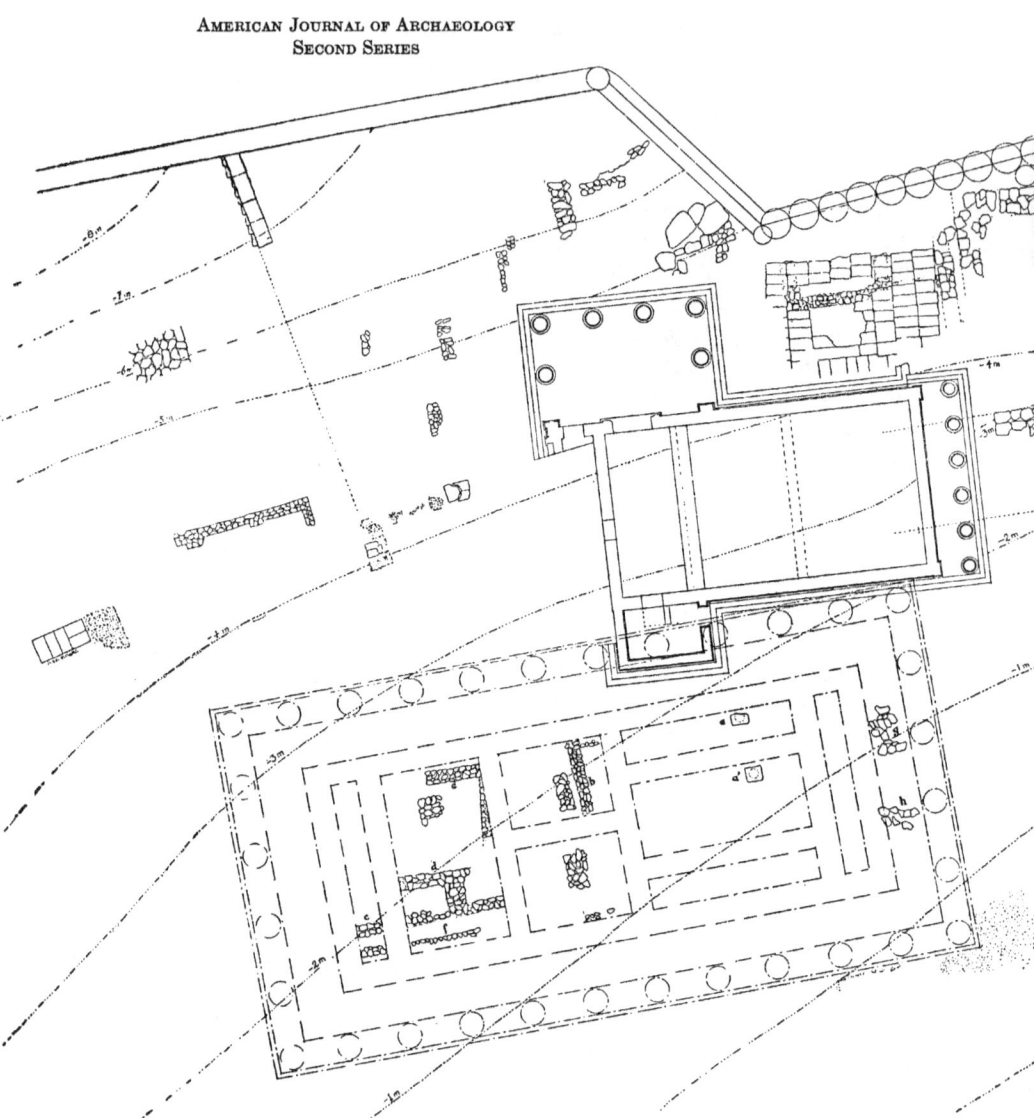

PREHISTORIC REMAINS IN THE

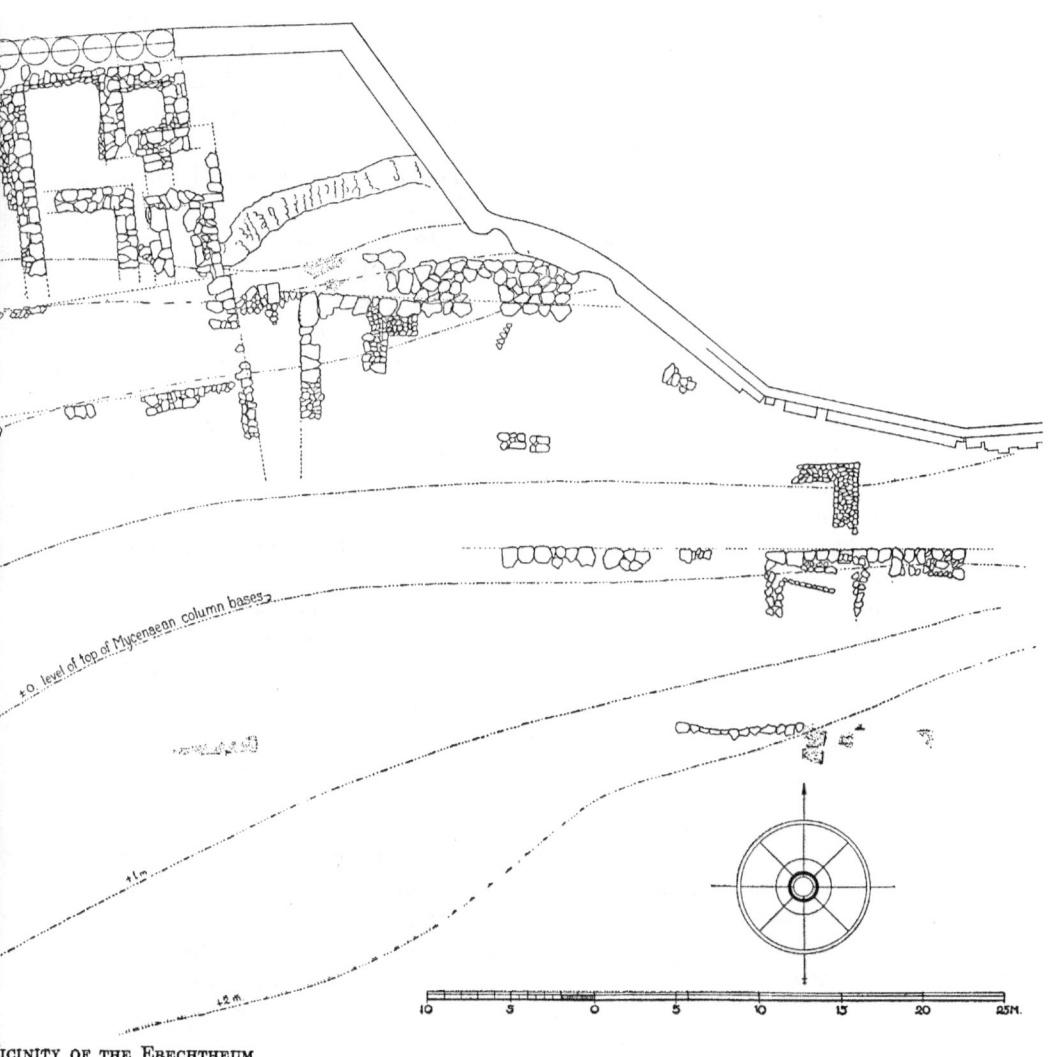

worth has been found there. Yet in the Geometric age, when the palace of Mycenae was a calcined ruin, great funeral vases from the Dipylon show that Athens was rich and had the cleverest craftsmen to be found in Greece.

As a result, the history of the Acropolis and of the buildings there is one of continued growth and gradual change. Alcmaeonidae and Pisistratidae might struggle among themselves for supremacy, but after all both parties were Athenians, whoever won there was no sack, no burning, no wholesale violence and since the days when Cecrops set the city there, there had been none, until the Persians came and burned it all.

There are two references to the Athenian citadel in the Homeric poems. First, in the *Iliad* (II, 549 ff.) we are told that "Athena settled Erechtheus in her own rich sanctuary, and there as the years go round the Athenian youths worship him with bulls and with lambs." Again in the *Odyssey* (VII, 78 ff.) it is stated that Athena went to Athens "and entered the strong house of Erechtheus." The first certainly appears to be an interpolation, the second may also be, but seems of older date. If they are interpolations the inference is this, that when the second was written there stood on the Acropolis a palace so venerable as to be called "the strong house of Erechtheus," with somewhere in its complex an unnamed shrine of Athena; while when the other was written, the prehistoric palace had disappeared and the cult of Erechtheus was continued in the now "rich temple of Athena." Later still Pausanias[1] tells us that in his time sacrifice to Erechtheus was made at an altar dedicated to Poseidon, in the building called the Erechtheum. Near the Erechtheum or on its site then, we should look for the remains of the "strong house of Erechtheus."

As a matter of fact, to the north and east of the classic building there are considerable remains of walls built of uncut Acropolis limestone, which in their technique are obviously Mycenaean (PLATE VII). At one time an entrance to the Acropolis lay here, the path leading up a narrow way between the rocks is still clearly visible; but when Themistocles or Cimon surrounded the citadel with poros walls, the grade was raised and the older work has, since that time, lain deep beneath the earth. It was brought to light by excavations on the Acropolis from 1885 to 1890, and where it seemed feasible, the old walls have been left exposed (Fig. 1). But the major part were covered up again and are only known to us in the plates published with the report of the excavations.[2] Fortunately the rubble walls were drawn at this point with unusual care; they give the impression of having been set down stone by stone, and where the

[1] I, 26, 5.
[2] Cavvadias und Kawerau, *Ausgrabung der Akropolis*, (to be referred to hereafter simply as Cavvadias) pls, Γ, Δ.

stones are still exposed they seem to agree perfectly with the published drawings. On the other hand, to the northwest and west of the Erechtheum, walls are shown upon the plans in quite a different way, the mechanical carelessness of which destroys all confidence in its accuracy. Many of the walls here are undoubtedly mediaeval, some are probably prehistoric, but there is no differentiation in the publication. A careful study on the ground might clear the matter

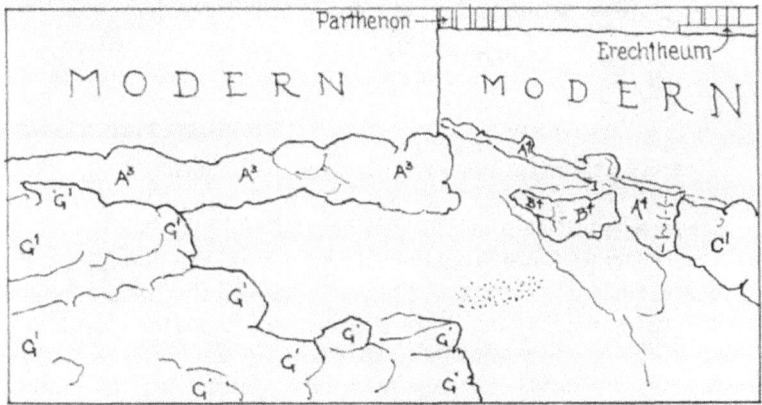

FIGURE 1.—PREHISTORIC REMAINS AT NORTHEAST ENTRANCE TO ACROPOLIS.
BELOW—KEY TO PHOTOGRAPH.

up, though the indications from potsherds which might have been had in 1885 are now quite gone. I have omitted from PLATE VII as dubious, most of the walls of Acropolis limestone to the west, but those to the northeast and east have been scrupulously copied. Walls of large stones, or small stone foundations for such walls, are surely prehistoric; walls of small stones, like that at the right hand of the plate, are probably mediaeval and have not been considered in the following discussion. Although it is hopeless now to attempt to date these walls by pottery, since the earth all about has been thoroughly disturbed (save in one locality, to be considered later), yet the sequence of their building and their function can be determined merely from their plan.

As one would expect, Greek prehistoric citadels were set upon the very summits of their hills, and, as they grew, in late Helladic times spread out around their nuclei on rectangular terraces clinging to the slopes. Until late Helladic III they seem often to have been unfortified. Just this condition is shown by Dr. Blegen's excavations at Zygouriés, where late Helladic houses lie along the edge of the village hill, upheld by terrace walls several metres high. At need these walls could serve for good defence, though not primarily built as fortifications. The four walls shown in black on Fig. 2 (compare PLATE VII) and marked A^1, A^2, A^3, A^4, seem to belong to early town terraces on the Athenian Acropolis. It will be noted

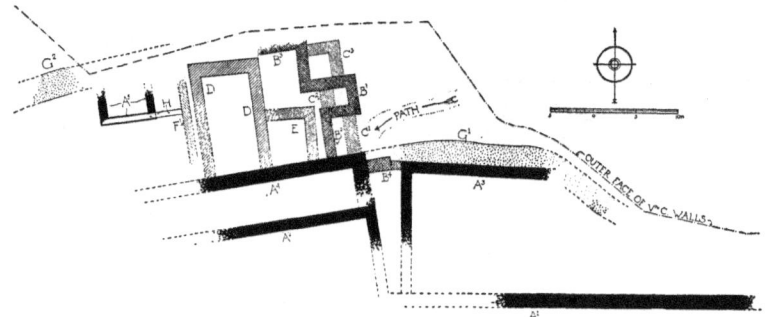

FIGURE 2.—PREHISTORIC WALLS NORTHEAST OF ERECHTHEUM.

that they roughly parallel the contours of the hill. Other similar terraces to the west probably once continued the circle round. The line of the ancient terrace wall that once flanked the Hecatompedon on the northwest, presumably ran parallel to the statue foundations shown at the extreme left of PLATE VII or to the north wall of the Pandroseum enclosure. It may also have determined the orientation of the rough rubble structure shown between these two. Of the terrace walls marked A, it may be that A^3 and A^4 are slightly later than A^1 and A^2, since they lie outside them. The east return of A^4 is not exactly continuous with that of A^2, suggesting a lack of contemporiety. A^3 was not continued to meet A^4, perhaps because of a desire for right angles to the terrace and the buildings built thereon, as well as in order to leave a gap for the drainage of water from the upper terraces. Gaps like this were found between the late Helladic houses along the hill at Zygouriés, and in them still lay terra-cotta drains. The little path which climbs up from the east ran along the foot of the terrace marked A^4. Perhaps it encircled all the north walls of the city of that time, on the level space between the contours marked −4 and −5 on PLATE VII, and led to a main western entrance way; or quicker access to the upper inner levels may have been gained at some nearer point, as, perhaps, where in classic days steps went up within the Erechtheum to the Porch of the Maidens.

Now the culture of the Achaean world[1] was not a peaceful one, and the terrace town of Athens found in time that it would be good to build a fortress gate to bar the northern entrance way. So a tower (B^1, Fig. 2) was placed opposite the northeast corner of the terrace A^4, and back between the two the gate B^2 was set. The west wall of the tower (C^2) does not bond with, and is thicker than the other walls. Probably it is a later addition, the tower originally being open in the rear, and hollow, with wooden floors. From the north side of the tower the wall ran west a little way, then north to the steep outer edge of the hill, then with another good rectangular bend, went west again (B^3) on approximately the line of the fifth century fortifications. The disposition of the gate is much like that of the Lions' Gate, or of the postern, at Mycenae. At this same time the drain way between A^4 and A^3 must have been blocked with a wall (B^4) of which only a few stones remain (see Fig. 1). The space behind may have been filled with earth or left open, but a drain probably still ran through. The appearance of the gateway at this period is shown in bird's-eye view, as seen, say, by Daedalus arriving by air from Sunium, in the sketch, Fig. 3.

But the storm clouds of invasion grew more threatening, and the little gate and curtain wall to the north were felt to be too vulnerable. So an unpierced wall (C^1) was built from the terrace A^4 across to the tower B^1 (see Fig. 1) and between it and the blocked up gate the space was filled with earth, to make a rampart here as solid as the tower, which at this time was walled across the rear (C^2) and filled with earth. Similarly in the northern corner a projecting right angle of wall (C^3) was built, and filled with earth to complete the massive barricade across the northeast path. These bits of wall do not bond in with walls A^4 and B; they are heavier than the walls B, and are always set back a little from the faces of walls they parallel. This can be clearly seen on the plan, and in reality where the stones are still exposed, and proves them to be subsequent in date.

Now when the gate was blocked, the path along the foot of terrace A^4 became no thoroughfare, so at some later period the rec-

[1] "Achaean" is used throughout as a rough chronological designation for the civilization in Greece shortly preceding the Dorian invasion. There is no attempt to imply any definite ethnic classification. (Compare J. P. Harland, 'Peloponessos in the Bronze Age,' *Harvard Studies in Classical Philology*, XXXIV, 1923, pp. 1 ff.)

FIGURE 3.—NORTHEAST ENTRANCE TO THE ACROPOLIS CA. 1400 B.C.

tangle D was built, which I presume, served to extend the level of the terrace A^4 to the north, and later still came E. If E was built as a terrace it seems very strange that it was not continued east to B^2–C^2; it looks, rather, as if E had been built so that the original low level could be reserved within it, to the southwest, while all the spaces between E and B to the east and north were filled, probably to the level of D and A^4. I have no guess as to why this should have been done here (see p. 159). The solid, earth-backed wall of terrace A^4 must have originally stood at least two metres high above the path, in order to have formed a proper flank to the gateway B^2, stone casemates, as at Tiryns might have carried the wall higher still. The earth level, then, would have come about to the level -1 shown on PLATE VII. In the middle of the fifth century the level to the east of the Erechtheum lay at about -1.10[1] so that it is probable that it had changed little from prehistoric times. The level east of the Hecatompedon was, throughout classic times, about $+0.25$, in prehistoric times it was a little lower. This would bring terrace A^2 about one metre above A^4. A^3 very likely corresponded with A^4, A^1 may have been on a level with A^2 or, perhaps, was somewhat higher.

FIGURE 4.—OLD WALL BENEATH POROS PAVEMENT, LOOKING NORTH.

When the fierce migrations of the Dorian tribes began, swamping the cities of the Achaean kings, Athens, though she stood aside from the main current of destruction, must have been troubled by the threat of doom; and waves of fugitives from barbarian wrath must have beat against her walls. So once again the fortifications were increased, and this time the work is of a new technique. These walls (G) are no longer straight, rectangular and only a metre to a metre and a half in thickness, but run in great continuous wandering curves around the citadel, the thickness varying from three metres up to five. This is the wall that formed a great looped bastion at

[1] 'Erechtheum Papers I,' *A. J. A.* XXVIII, p. 21, and note 1.

the southeast corner of the Acropolis (see Cavvadias, *op. cit.* pl. A) and ran by the southwest angle of the Parthenon. In both places bits of it can still be seen. It is the wall which flanked the western gateway on the site of the present Propylaea, straight here for the only stretch of its circumference, and full six metres thick. At this point once it rose at least nine metres high on the outer side, and four metres of it still are left. Presumably it is the wall called by the classic Greeks "Pelasgian," and as it seems so different from the earlier Athenian walls there may be more than fable in the story of another race that built it. At any rate a piece of it (G^1)

FIGURE 5.—OLD WALL BENEATH POROS PAVEMENT, LOOKING EAST.

still lies along the outside of terrace A^3 where it more than doubled the original thickness of the wall (see Fig. 1). The gateway wall north from the northeast corner of A^4, being already doubled, seems to have been considered strong enough, for there is no new construction here; but from the north side of B^3 the new wall probably continued west on the line of the present poros wall, being quite removed when the latter was built. Northeast of the north porch of the Erechtheum (PLATE VII) there is a small group of very massive stones which probably belonged to it (G^2), but westward from this point again its course is lost. It may have followed the contour line -5 and turned sharply north where a scrap of it seems still to lie, (on contour -6) and it appears again to the west of the postern stairs in the fifth century wall (Cavvadias *op. cit.* pl. Γ marked 12.).

So, having weathered the Dorian invasion, it seems that Athens built no further defenses to the upper town,—though later lighter walls, of course, enclosed the growing city on the slopes and at the foot of the Acropolis,—until the Persian sack and flames made

FIGURE 6.—OLD WALL BENEATH POROS PAVEMENT, LOOKING SOUTHWEST.

necessary a whole new ring. These new walls, elegantly built of well-cut poros, simplified and extended the circuit of the Pelasgian curves. The whole reëntrant corner outside the prehistoric postern gate was enclosed in high straight walls, and all the space within filled to the level of the terrace A^4, and by this act the strong gateway to the house of Erechtheus has been preserved to us. It may well be also, that the section north of contour −5 (PLATE VII) and east of the scrap of Pelasgian wall on contour −6 was first included in the Acropolis at that time.

Between the Erechtheum and the northern wall lies an area

which was paved, in the fifth century, with large blocks of poros. At some time in the Middle Ages a number of blocks from the centre of this area had been removed, and digging in this open space the excavators of 1885–1890 laid bare a prehistoric wall. This wall was measured and drawn and then the hole refilled. But the masonry as shown by Cavvadias (*op. cit.* pl. Γ) does not seem quite so carefully drawn here as it is further east, and since the wall might conceivably have some relation to the pre-Erechtheum or to the gate, it seemed worth while in the spring of 1923 to open up the hole again.[1]

FIGURE 7.—SOUTHEAST CORNER OF EXCAVATION IN PAVED AREA.

It was found that the earlier excavators had gone down practically to bed rock throughout the open area, though in some places hollows held a few centimetres of undisturbed earth. In one such hollow, just north of the centre of the ancient wall, a fragment of an infant's skull was found. The earth from the refilling contained sherds of pottery of every period, from late prehistoric down to mediaeval. There were also a few fragments of very well made roof-tiles and of a terra-cotta sima painted with a tongue leaf pattern above and a simple guilloche below. The only color used on it is Indian red against the yellow-buff background; the style would indicate that

[1] I am very much indebted to Mr. Wace of the British School and to Dr. Blegen of the American School for their critical advice during this excavation, and for invaluable assistance in dating the pottery.

it was made at the end of the sixth or beginning of the fifth century B.C. The pattern is not exactly like any in the Acropolis Museum.

The ancient wall (Figs. 4, 5 and 6) was found to be moderately well built of uncut blocks of Acropolis limestone, from 30 to 50 cm. in their largest dimensions, laid in roughly horizontal courses, occasionally on bed rock but for the most part on a few centimetres of hard earth. No clay and few small stones were used to fill the spaces in the wall, as was often done in Mycenaean work. The main section of the wall runs roughly east and west; two or three courses 75 cm.

FIGURE 8.—NORTH END OF EAST WALL BENEATH POROS BLOCKS, SHOWING FLOOR TO RIGHT.

wide bring it to a total height of 40–80 cm. above bed rock. Remains of a top course approximately 20 cm. high and 55 cm. wide exist in places—two stones at the extreme west end (Fig. 6), a small patch about the middle (Figs. 4, 5, and 6), and a few more stones at the east (Figs. 5 and 7) partially beneath the poros blocks. This top course is more carefully laid than those below, with straight north and south faces; the poros blocks come directly on top of it. It seems certain that when the poros was laid the old wall stood higher than it now does, and was leveled down to receive the pavement. At the west end the wall turned north (Figs. 4 and 6); so far as can be ascertained it ran no farther west or south, but the north extension continued on beneath the poros pavement and can be identified again at the northern edge of the latter. This part

FIGURE 9.—MYCENAEAN WALL EAST OF POROS PAVEMENT, LOOKING NORTH.

of the ancient wall is as was shown by Cavvadias, but at the eastern end of the open area also it turns to the north (Figs. 5 and 7), and this detail has not been shown. The north end of this wing, too, can be clearly identified at the northern edge of the poros area (Fig. 8). But curiously enough the top course of the wall does not seem to turn here at the eastern end of the open pit, but runs on east beneath the poros (Fig. 7). The eastern edge of the poros area comes close against another ancient wall (Fig. 9, labelled F^1, Fig. 2) of well laid Acropolis limestone, the top of which is now about flush with the poros pavement and which runs parallel to and close beside the western face of terrace D. Scratching in the narrow space between the poros and this wall was very difficult, but enough could be done to find there the eastern continuation of the old wall beneath the poros (Fig. 9). The stones here were small and poorly laid and were unmistakably set against wall F^1 after the latter had been built (for accurate plan, see Fig. 12).

Although the open space in the pavement had been excavated once or twice before, the earth beneath the poros blocks themselves had not been disturbed since these were laid, so that it was possible here, and, perhaps, here only on the Acropolis, to date positively a prehistoric wall. On carefully shaving down the earth along the north face of the hole[1] it was found that directly beneath the poros blocks were five to ten centimetres of poros chips (Fig. 4), then small stones, then ill-distinguished layers of earth down to a depth of 55 cm. below the bottom of the poros blocks. At this point

FIGURE 10.—NORTHEAST CORNER OF EXCAVATION IN PAVED AREA, SHOWING FLOOR.

there was a clear line of white clay about $2\frac{1}{2}$ cm. thick (Fig. 10). Bed rock lay 10–15 cm. lower still. The layer of clay was undoubtedly a floor; it was found to run right up to the east face of the west wall and to the west face of the east wall, both in the main excavation within the poros area, and in those which laid bare the ends of these walls to the north of the poros blocks (Fig. 8). In every place it was found at a depth of 50–55 cm. below the bottom of the poros blocks, though the bed rock dropped away at least 40 cm. in its slope from southeast to northwest. Beneath the poros at the northwest corner of the main hole a sort of basin had been made in the clay floor (Fig. 11). It was surrounded by a rectangular rim

[1] I have to thank Dr. R. R. Rosborough of the American Academy in Rome for much assistance in this work.

of the same white clay, 5½ cm. wide by 3 cm. high. No trace of any floor could be found outside of the enclosure formed by the main wall and the eastern and western wings, neither to the east nor to the west nor south.

Throughout the earth below the poros blocks there were sparse scraps of pottery, and these were remarkably uniform in character.[1] Only one small scrap was found which could have been earlier than the middle Helladic period. There was a little gray Minyan ware, more yellow Minyan, and a fair amount of unpolished yellowish-

FIGURE 11.—NORTHWEST CORNER OF EXCAVATION IN PAVED AREA, SHOWING RAISED CLAY RIM IN FLOOR.

green ware sometimes sparingly decorated with dark matt paint. The predominant ware, however, was of a well-made polished fabric, like yellow Minyan, but salmon-red in color. Many fragments came from pots of characteristic late Helladic I shapes. Only a few pieces decorated with glazed paint were found, these dated from late Helladic I or some, perhaps, from late Helladic II. Nowhere was there anything later, save for one or two classic fragments, probably intrusions from the previous refilling of the excavation.

The floor seems to be certainly contemporary with the walls, and as the pottery was the same above as below the floor, the whole construction should date from the very end of the middle Helladic period or the early part of the late Helladic period. That is, ac-

[1] For a detailed study of the types of pottery here mentioned see Blegen, *Korakou*.

cording to Blegen's chronology[1] about 1600–1500 B.C. There can be no doubt that the main wall and the east and west walls enclosed a room, which ran north presumably, to about the line of the present and earlier Pelasgian fortifications, beyond which point the grade drops very steeply down.[2] The child's skull found beneath the floor, dates probably from the period of habitation of this room, and marks it as a dwelling house.[3] The absence of any floor to the south suggests that there was a street or open piece of ground there instead of any building. But the continuation of the main wall east until it hits wall F^1 presents a difficulty. Judging by its excellent construction it is hard to believe that the latter is any

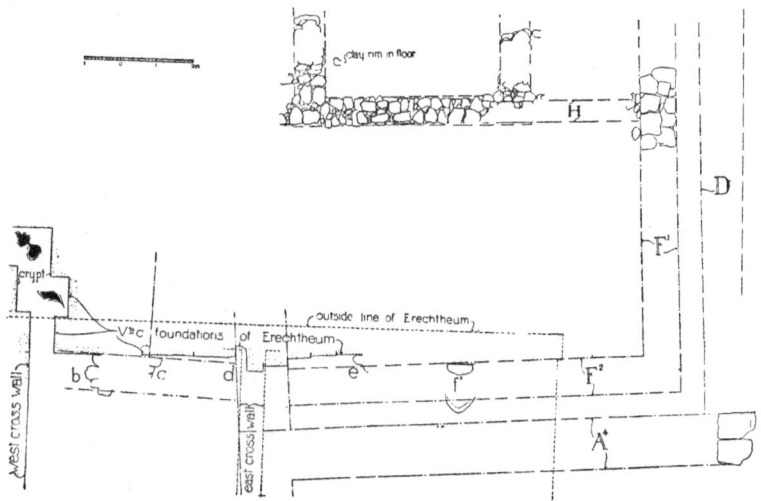

FIGURE 12.—SCHEMATIC PLAN OF PREHISTORIC THEATRAL AREA.

earlier than late Helladic III, some two centuries after the date assigned to the clay-floored room, yet it seemed beyond dispute that the eastern continuation of the older main wall was laid against wall F^1. The only explanation that I can see is, that the wall beneath the area of poros blocks is of two periods. First we have the lower courses of the main wall and the east and west wings, beyond which the main wall did not originally run, all belonging to a house of the very beginning of the late Helladic period (A^5, Fig. 2 and Fig. 12). This house was probably not used as such for long, since

[1] *Korakou*, pp. 120 ff.
[2] Blegen's excavations at Korakou have shown that the houses of the Middle Helladic period were long and narrow with absidal ends (*Korakou*, pp. 76 ff.), presumably with "hoop roofs." (Holland, *A. J. A.* XXIV, 1920, p. 326.) The houses of the Late Helladic period were regularly rectangular and had flat roofs. Just how or when the change took place we do not yet know, but it would seem that the latter type was used in Athens, at least as early as the beginning of L. H. I.
[3] Intramural burials of childrenw ere common in Middle Helladic times, but seem to have been abandoned later (see Harland, *op. cit.* p. 15).

the earth within its walls must have filled up very rapidly to contain pottery of such uniform style clear up to the under surface of the paved area, 55 cm. above the floor. At the time wall F^1 was built the grade probably stood somewhere between the top and bottom of the poros blocks. Then, toward the end of late Helladic III, or possibly even somewhat later, I surmise that a second wall was built upon the line of the old main wall (H, Figs. 2 and 12). To this second construction belong the few stones referred to as an upper course. It was continued eastward till it met wall F^1 and possibly westward also beyond the western wall, though it seems more likely to have turned north on top of this.

As an interpretation of the functions of all the walls in this section I suggest the following (Fig. 2).

The terrace A^4 continued west beyond the east face of the Erechtheum. On PLATE VII, copied from Cavvadias' plan, it seems to stop short at that line, but photographs taken at the time of the excavations show that actually the foundations of the east porch extend more than a metre east of the superstructure, and that the prehistoric wall was intersected by them. Probably A^4 continued all across the eastern cella of the Erechtheum and at the west was ended by a wall returning at right angles approximately on the line of the classic east cross wall. To the north of A^4 ran the path which climbed the Acropolis from the east and which broadened out into a little plaza on the relatively level ground where later the paved area lay. At the north of this plaza the clay-floored house was built (A^5, Fig. 2) with walls of unbaked brick on a low base wall of stone. When the gate and northern walls,—probably somewhat later than the house,—were built, the open plaza inside lay in much the same relative position as the open area of the grave circle at Mycenae inside the Lions' Gate. Then, as we have seen, when the gate was abandoned and built across, the terrace or group of buildings on the terrace D flanked the plaza on the east, as A^4 did along the southern side. Then I imagine comes wall F^1. This might conceivably be the east wall of some structure lying to the west of D with a narrow space left between the adjacent walls, but such a structure should have left some traces in the open space of the poros area where the remains of the house A^5 were found. The continuation of the later wall H up against wall F^1 also argues against its having formed part of any structure lying to the west. And it is too close to D to have belonged to a corridor along its flank. (See Fig. 9, where the face of the modern wall at the extreme right of the picture is built very nearly on the line of the western face of D.)

An explanation is suggested by the prehistoric remains within the Erechtheum; it seems to me the only plausible one. Here, it was shown[1] that a Mycenaean wall, lying just inside the classic north foundations, carried a paved way along its top at the time the late fifth century Erechtheum was begun. Now a line parallel to A^4 through the northern edge of stone e (Fig. 12 and 'Erechtheum Papers I', A pl. I, *A. J. A.* XXVIII, No. 1) conforms nicely to the offsets of the irregular poros foundations just to the west. This line would correspond to the footings of the older wall to which e belonged. The upper part, as indicated by the foundations of the Erechtheum, was set back somewhat to the south; so the northern face should lie a few centimetres north of the north face of f^2 (Fig. 12, and 'Erechtheum Papers I', pl. I, A and B), a distance of about 1.65 m. north of the western continuation of A^4. This agrees as exactly as such measurements can, with the distance from the western face of F^1 to D, and hence it seems reasonable to conclude that F^1 and F^2 (the wall within the Erechtheum) were similar, and were both built to carry narrow terrace walks along the base of the higher terraces that flanked the plaza on the east and south. In support of this it should be noted that the western face of F^1 is better laid and brought more accurately to a line (Figs. 9 and 12) than is the eastern one, which would, of course, be hidden by fill. If the level of the plaza were that of the top of the poros pavement blocks, then the terrace walks would lie about a metre and a half above, and the larger terraces about three-quarters of a metre higher still. According to this hypothesis the plaza had now evidently become a sort of theatral area, recalling on a modest scale the areas for public spectacles, paved and flanked on two adjoining sides by tiers of steps, which have been found in Crete in connection with the palaces of Cnossus and Phaestus.

But what of the house A^5? It does not seem likely that it ever wholly disappeared, since its walls served as foundations for the later wall H, and yet from the rate at which the fill of earth accumulated within, it hardly seems possible that it could have continued as a house. My surmise is that when D was built, if not before, the house ceased to be a house and was partially pulled down and partially filled up to form an isolated terrace, in function like the bastion at the southeast corner of the theatral area at Cnossus. Perhaps a shrine stood upon it, or perhaps more likely it served as a "royal box." Perhaps another bit of terrace walk ran along the inside of the north fortification walls, to connect it with F^1, and it is probably significant that while the west wall of D is not parallel to the east wall, nor at right angles with its own north wall nor with A^4 on the south, yet both it and F^1 are in astonishing accord with the lines of A^5 (Figs. 2 and 12). It is quite possible, of course, that F^1 and F^2 were built at the same time as D. They are all certainly

[1] 'Erechtheum Papers I,' *A. J. A.* XXVIII p. 11.

later than A^4. In any case, at some period after the terrace walks F^1 and F^2 had been built, the isolated northern terrace was extended eastward for its full width till it joined F^1, thus enclosing the theatral area on three sides with continuous galleries for the spectators.

To the east and west of the old side walls of the house A^5, beneath the poros blocks, there seemed to be a good many loose stones of the size of those in the walls. These may have come from a lowering of these walls at an early date. It is to be noted that no such stones are found in the undisturbed earth within the area of the house. To the south, of course, any such tumbled stones, if ever there, have long since been removed. But just to the south of the ancient wall, beneath the poros blocks at the west of the hole in the pavement, there is first a layer 40 cm. deep of fairly hard, reddish brown earth, then 30 cm. of hard light-colored clay, and then a hard and apparently virgin layer of decayed stone. The upper red-brown earth might well be disintegrated unbaked brick from the house, dumped on the ground outside when the level there lay some 15 cm. above the level of the floor within.

At the west, the theatral area must have been limited by a construction of which there are now no traces whatsoever, but the existence of which can be deduced as follows. In the roof of the North Porch of the classic Erechtheum there was left, intentionally, a hole; approximately beneath this hole there was an opening in the floor and underneath the floor a crypt (Fig. 12), entered from the western cella by a little door in the foundations.[1] Except for this curiously shaped crypt the North Porch is supported on a solid platform of poros blocks. Now, in the native rock floor of the crypt are five peculiar holes deeply drilled in the rock by primeval waters. (Three of them are shown in Fig. 12.) It is universally assumed that there was some relation between these marks and the openings in the porch above. Some consider the marks to be the work of Poseidon's trident, others, damage caused by the thunderbolt which slew Erechtheus. In either case they would have been of very venerable antiquity to the classic Athenian. But as we have seen, the level of the area lying just to the east of the North Porch was already up to the bottom of the poros pavement there, by the fourteenth century B.C. That is, it was at least 50 cm. above the level of the rock where the god-made holes occur. In early classic times we should expect it to be considerably higher. So, unless the marks were only first revealed when the earth was cleared away down to the native rock, to lay the foundations of the North Porch,—in which case we should hardly expect them to have been considered sufficiently sacred to warrant openings in the

[1] 'Erechtheum Papers I,' *A. J. A.* XXVIII p. 3, and fig. 1.

floor and roof above,—then we must assume that from a very early, even prehistoric date some coffer-dam of stone, perhaps like E, Fig. 2 (see p. 145) had kept the rock face free from invasion by the higher earth around. Of course the foundations of the North Porch and the mediaeval cisterns built between it and the poros pavement have effectually destroyed all traces of any such retaining wall, but a hint of it may lie in the Mycenaean remains within the Erechtheum.

Our investigation so far has indicated that just within the classic foundations of the eastern cella stood a low terrace wall F^2 parallel to the hypothetical western half of A^4. But where the classic east cross wall lies, two of the foundation blocks project farther south than the north face of F^2 (Fig. 12). Just west of them there is a deep cut d, evidently for the projection of some prehistoric block northward beyond the presumed face of the lower terrace wall F^2. It seems obvious, therefore, that the wall which bounds the upper terrace A^4 at its western end, extended north, at least in its lower part, beyond A^4 across the west end of the lower terrace, and was continued even farther than the north face of F^2. The purpose might have been to form a cheek for a ramp or flight of steps leading up to the terrace walk, or to the area in the west cella of the Erechtheum. The stone that filled the cut at d would probably lie on the line of the western face of the west wall of terrace A^4. The northern wall of A^4 seems to have been about 1.40 m. thick. If the west wall were the same, its cut north end would fill the cavity at d and abut against the two southward projecting poros blocks just to the east. East of this point the foundations follow evenly the line assumed for the footings of the wall F^2. If terrace A^4 ended in an accurate right angle, then the west face of the prehistoric west wall would lie at its northern end about 15 cm. west of the west face of the classic cross wall, and 15 cm. west of the east face of the latter at its southern end.

Now if the line of the wall F^2 be continued west of this cross wall it comes well south of the inner face of the classic foundations; and in truth, the foundations here were not set as if to abut against an ancient wall. But further west again (see 'Erechtheum Papers I', fig. 4) one prehistoric stone c^1 projects north into a cutting in the poros like that at d, and further still b^1 (*ibid*. fig. 5) has been trimmed as if the original north face of the old wall at this point had lain just a little further north. Either, then, there must have been a break in the line or an offset at this point, or the wall in the western cella bore no relation to F^2 in the east. The way the stones at b and c are laid seems to me to indicate the latter (Fig. 12). Thus c^1 and c^3 seem to have belonged to a reëntrant angle between two walls, c^3 lying in the north face of the one running roughly east and west. If a line be drawn along this face it will pass just north of the north face of b^1 and at the east will hit the west wall of the terrace walk just about where the line of F^2 also intersects it. c^1 would then belong to a wall running northward, at right angles to this wall, perhaps the other cheek of the ramp or stairs suggested by the north projection of the wall at d, or perhaps the eastern wall of the area inclosing the holy drill-holes of the gods. The possibilities here are too numerous to warrant much assurance in any particular restoration.

So far we have found sufficient evidence to establish a consistent even if hypothetical reconstruction of a fortified gateway to the house of Erechtheus and his heirs, and of an area where councils may have met or sacred rites or dances have been held, and probably the phrase "house of Erechtheus" should include all these and many other elements, just as the palaces at Tiryns and Mycenae hold very many different rooms and corridors and courts. But the heart of a proper Achaean palace is the great hall or megaron, and certainly nothing of that sort ever lay within the areas which have so far been scrutinized. If any traces of a great hall still exist they are to be found among the foundations of the sixth century structure commonly called the Hecatompedon.

The survey and plan of this building were made by Professor Doerpfeld and appeared first in the *Antike Denkmaeler*, I, pl. I. The same plan is reproduced by Wiegand.[1] Between the foundations of the sixth century building the plan shows certain bits of rubble wall; one of these just north of the south wall of the western cella is labelled "*Späteres Verstärkung*," another bit just inside the east peristyle is labelled "*Späteres Mauerwerk*," and a similar scrap just south apparently belongs to the same category. And there are three bits of rubble in the two small central rooms which are unlabelled. The plan of Cavvadias[2] reproduces that of Doerpfeld scrupulously, but additional rubble walls are shown, two in the rear pronaos and four or five in the western cella. These as well as the earlier ones are here all unlabelled. But Wiegand[3] gives also a later plan by Doerpfeld. Here there are a few new stones in the masonry of the Hecatompedon, and all the bits of rubble in Cavvadias' plan are shown, with very minor variations, but the drawing seems somewhat more schematic than in the earlier work. The rubble bits are lettered b, c, d, e, f, g, h. On my own PLATE VII, I have shown them as does Cavvadias, with emendations and letters according to Doerpfeld's latest plan. Two in the western cella and two in the small inner rooms have no letters, they are shown as being built of somewhat larger stones than the lettered bits. Somewhere I presume, Professor Doerpfeld intended to discuss these

---

[1] *Die Archaische Poros-Architektur der Akropolis zu Athen*, abb. 72.
[2] *Op. cit.* pl. Γ.   [3] *Op. cit.* abb. 117.

fragmentary rubble walls, but all he says[1] is, that the majority are older than the temple and belong either to an older temple or to dwellings, though some fragments seem to be mediaeval. If the lettered bits are preclassic then Professor Doerpfeld must have changed his mind about those marked f and g, which were labelled "*Spätere*" in the *Antike Denkmaeler* plan. But if the lettered ones be mediaeval, then the rubble walls which are older than the temple are certainly not in the majority. If they actually run under the sixth century walls,—unfortunately they are mostly covered now and reëxcavation would be necessary to determine this,—they are certainly prehistoric, but I should think would lie at a considerably lower level, and, therefore, be older than the column bases (a and a[1]) to be shortly discussed. Otherwise the lettered fragments must all be mediaeval, for if the classic walls had intersected the lines of earlier walls the latter would surely have been pulled away and the small stones removed for a space on either side of the line of the newer walls, so that the latter might be properly laid. But all the lettered walls run close against the classic ones, thus indicating that they were built against them at a later date. This leaves only the two unlettered bits in the centres of the two small inner rooms,—which might reasonably be parts of an older wall cut by the median wall of the classic building,—and two rather vaguely square unlettered bits in the western cella. These last I suspect were really foundations for the bases of columns in the classic building, for unless the western cella was unroofed it surely must have had interior supports.[2]

Now in the eastern cella lie two square cut blocks of poros with raised circular surfaces on the upper side (a and a[1], PLATE VII). These were unquestionably bases for wooden columns, and have every appearance of being Mycenaean. Since the dating of the

[1] *Wiegand, op. cit.* p. 117.
[2] In accordance with normal Greek practice the roof was probably carried on a longitudinal ridge and purlins parallel to it. In the eastern cella the ridge would be carried on heavy ceiling beams spanning transversely from row to row of columns, the purlins would come directly above these rows. Continuing westward across the two small rooms, the purlins would be carried on transverse ceiling beams with a span equal to that of those in the eastern cella; the ridge would be carried on the median wall. The only logical arrangement for the western cella is to duplicate that in the eastern one, and as the room is shallow, single columns, probably of wood, would serve to carry wooden architraves from east to west, on which the transverse ceiling timbers would be borne. The spans of the architraves would be about 3 m. in the clear. The length of the east cella is 10.50 m., so it is possible that there were only two columns in each row there, instead of three as restored by Doerpfeld. (*Antike Denkmaeler* I, pl. I). The span, a little over three metres, would of course require architraves of wood, and the columns would probably be of wood also. It may be that these were later replaced by stone columns, three to a row instead of two. No remains of these interior columns seem to have been found, Doerpfeld says of them (Wiegand, *op. cit.* p. 119), "*es lässt sich aus der Breite der Stylobate auch entnehmen, dass diese Innensäulen viel dünner waren, als diejenigen der äusseren Halle; allein die Zahl der Säulen und ihre Form ist vollständig unbestimmt.*" May this not be because they were of wood?

bits of rubble wall is so uncertain, these two column bases, and possibly the two broken bits of wall in the small inner rooms, are all we have with which to reconstruct the great hall of the Athenian kings. And even so the column bases may never have belonged to a megaron, but to a propylon, as in the palace at Tiryns, or again as at Tiryns, they might have stood in a colonnaded court. However, since in classic times a monumental building occupied this site, while apparently no gate stood anywhere nearby, the continuity of Athenian development argues in favor of a megaron rather than a propylon, and the little town seems hardly important enough to have afforded the luxury of a colonnaded court when great Mycenae had none.

The arrangements of the megara at Tiryns and Mycenae are the same, in each there are three pairs of columns, a first pair in the portico and two more pairs in the great hall behind. The transverse distance, on centres, between the columns of each pair is, at Tiryns about four metres, at Mycenae about four metres and a half. The distance on centres, between the front and rear pairs within the great halls, is at Tiryns very nearly five metres and a quarter, and at Mycenae just about five metres. The clear span of the architraves is, of course, reduced in all cases by the diameter of the columns, roughly half a metre. Now at Athens the column bases are, on centres, only 3.31 m. apart. Therefore, unless the megaron at Athens was very much smaller than the other two, we must conclude that this is the shorter transverse interaxial width, and that the main axis of the hall ran east and west. The other megara give no help in this question of orientation, for that at Tiryns faces south and that at Mycenae west. We have here then, a megaron of which the relative width is as 3.00 to 3.50 and to 4.00 compared with those at Tiryns and Mycenae. A tabulation of the other dimensions of the two known megara will enable us to determine within reasonable limits dimensions[1] proportionally proper for the one at Athens.

	Tiryns	Mycenae
Transverse span between columns, clear	3.40 m.	3.90 m.
Longitudinal span between columns, clear	4.75	4.40
Transverse span from columns to walls, clear	2.60	3.25
Longitudinal span from columns to walls, clear	2.90	3.60
Longitudinal depth of vestibule, clear	4.75	4.35
Longitudinal depth of portico, columns to wall, clear	3.65	2.85
Thickness of walls	1.05–1.65	0.90

It is evident that Tiryns is the more daring building, with somewhat greater longitudinal spans and with much heavier walls. In

[1] In calculating analogous proportions as is done here, minute dimensions are, of course, useless, so that the dimensions at Tiryns and Mycenae have been approximated with units of not less than .05 m. and at Athens of not less than .25 m.

transverse development it seems to have been restricted by the exigencies of an already built up site. Mycenae's megaron on the other hand, was set on a made plateau, supported by a terrace wall along one side and in the rear. Therefore granted the skill, by no means slight, required to build the terrace wall at all on a very steep incline, the architect was free to make the dimensions of his hall a metre or so, more or less, at will. The relative proportions at Mycenae should then be more typical than those at Tiryns. The spans of the vestibule and of the interior columns from front to rear seem to be in each case the maxima that the builders dared.

Assuming the dimensions at Athens to have been approximately three-fourths as great as those at Mycenae, since the span between columns in the clear is just about 3.00 m. and 4.00 m. we get:

	MYCENAE	ATHENS
Transverse span between columns, clear	4.00 m.	3.00 m.
Longitudinal span between columns, clear	4.40	3.25
Transverse span from columns to walls, clear	3.25	2.50
Longitudinal span from columns to walls, clear	3.60	2.75
Longitudinal depth of vestibule, clear	4.35	3.25
Longitudinal depth of portico, columns to wall, clear	2.85	2.25

The thickness of the walls can hardly have been less than 0.90 m. in any case.

Therefore if the columns at Athens belonged to a megaron at all, we can be fairly certain that the dimensions of the building did not depart materially from those given above, that is to say, the probable error can hardly be greater in any case than 50 cm., and in most cases it is presumably less.

However, with these same dimensions there are six possible positions in which the hall could be reconstructed around the column bases. The latter might have belonged to the columns in the portico, or to the front or rear pair in the interior, and the hall may have faced either east or west. If they were in the portico of a megaron facing west, then the front wall of the vestibule would have very nearly coincided with the east wall of the east cella of the Hecatompedon (see PLATE VII) and the rear wall of the vestibule with the foundations of the front of the later pronaos. The absence of any remains of these two early walls would thus be well explained. The south wall of the megaron would have lain close enough to the foundations of the south row of columns of the Hecatompedon to account for the disappearance of its western end; the space between the front and rear foundations of the pronaos is so restricted that we should not expect any traces there, and across the later peristyle the wall would have come at a point where now many of the stones of the Hecatompedon itself have disappeared, so that the disappearance of earlier stones would not be surprising. The north wall would have lain between the north wall of the east cella of the Hecatompedon and the foundations of the Pisistratid peristyle. The latter are carried down to solid rock, and when they were being built any rubble walls north of the cella wall would probably have been removed. But the rear part of a megaron in this assumed position would have projected well out into the open space east of the Hecatompedon, where no remains at all are shown by Cavvadias. Of course prehistoric walls here might have been so involved with mediaeval constructions that the excavators failed to recognize them and did not put them on their plan, but their absence therefrom is certainly a good negative argument against this position for the megaron. If we consider the column bases to have been for the *front* pair of interior columns of a megaron facing west, then no part would have projected east of the Hecatompedon, and the north and south walls will have lain as in the first position, where they would probably have been removed for the most part. But the west end of the southern wall would have projected far enough into the small south room of the Hecatompedon to render some remains of it probable. The rear columns would have come in the pronaos and the rear wall in the area of the eastern peristyle, where remains of it, in the northern part at least, might be expected. The front wall of the vestibule would have coincided approximately, with the rear wall of the cella of the Hecatompedon, but the rear wall would have run clear across the open cella. Since there is no trace of it, this position can reasonably be rejected. If the bases had been for the *rear* columns in a megaron facing west, the rear wall would have coincided with the east wall of the later cella, and the front wall with the rear wall of the latter. The front wall of the vestibule might have come where the bits of rubble stone work lie in the two small inner rooms; the portico columns would have come on the east wall of the western cella, and the west column bases, lying within the east cella of the Hecatompedon, might easily have disappeared. In fact it is very much more surprising that the two bases now *in situ*, useful poros blocks of convenient size, should have remained, than that others should have been removed.[1] But the west end of the south wall would have lain right across the centre of the southern inner room of the Hecatompedon. It should have crossed the bit of rubble stone work there, and as there is no trace of it we can reject this arrangement too.

Of possible positions facing east, that with the column bases in the portico would bring the south wall not only across the southern inner room but into the west cella of the Hecatompedon, and the

[1] There is another Mycenaean column base at present lying loose, to the northeast of the Erechtheum. It is of a hard greenish stone instead of poros, and its exact provenance seems to be unknown. It probably did not belong to the same structure as the poros bases, but, perhaps, came from some vanished propylon.

rear wall of the megaron would have run from north to south full in the open there. Assuming them to have been for the *rear* columns of the megaron brings the rear wall of the latter across the eastern cella, and projects the portico eastward beyond the eastern peristyle. But if they be taken as belonging to the *front* interior columns of the megaron, the agreement of the earlier with the later walls is almost perfect. The only place where traces of prehistoric walls might have been left, is where the south wall would have crossed the pronaos and peristyle; even here the chances of preservation would, as we have seen, have been very slight. The

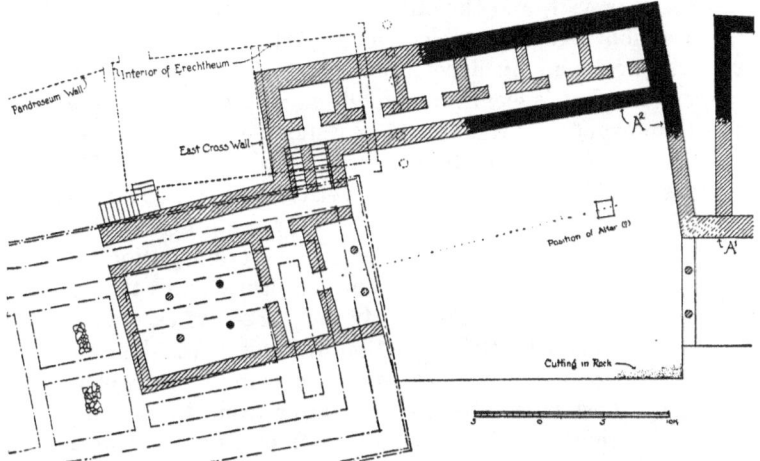

FIGURE 13.—RESTORED PLAN OF MEGARON SOUTH OF ERECHTHEUM.

western column bases alone are missing, but that, too, need not astonish us.

So if there ever was a megaron here, as is commonly supposed, to which these column bases once belonged, it follows almost necessarily that it lay as in Fig. 13, and was of approximately the size there shown. The orientation, fixed by the column bases, is between that of the walls A^2–A^4 and the line of the Pandroseum enclosure, which was probably dictated by former terrace walls west of the megaron. To the north there must have been a retaining wall on approximately the line of the Pisistratid peristyle; this would have served as the terrace wall for the cella of the Hecatompedon until superseded by the Pisistratid construction. Between this north wall and the megaron there is room for a passage like that behind the megaron at Tiryns. Perhaps, where the Porch of the Maidens now lies, a stair led up from the lower level.

A court should lie in front of a megaron. Here this would probably be bounded on the north by the line of A^2 and would be flanked there by buildings on the terrace A^4. It has been assumed that A^4 lies a metre or so below the level of the column bases, and consequently is that depth below the level of the court; there is sufficient room between the western wall of A^4 and the façade of the megaron to allow for a stairway leading down to the level of the terrace A^4 and another leading up, a metre or two, to a second story above magazines, like those at Tiryns, which may have been built thereon. The eastern limit of the court is fixed by the eastern return of A^2, about 24 m. east of the megaron. The court at Mycenae is only 13 m. deep; the court at Tiryns in front of the great megaron is about 17 m. to the face of the colonnade, or nearly 20 m. to the rear wall, and the outer court there was at least 25 m. in each direction. It is possible that at Athens the east side of the court was occupied by a colonnade or by buildings of which no trace remains, but it seems more likely that it was merely somewhat larger than usual. And it should be remembered that the Acropolis at Athens is one-quarter larger than that at Tiryns. There are no stones at all left to mark the southern boundary, but still there is a possible reconstruction there, that is very tempting. The eastern wall, A^2, probably ran south until it met the prolongation westward of A^1. At both Tiryns and Mycenae the propylon to the court lies on the side facing the megaron. If that were the case here too, it must have lain south of the junction of A^2 and A^1. The propylon would probably be rectangular and be oriented by A^1 which would form its northern side. Now a line drawn from the intersection of A^2 and A^1 at right angles to the latter, comes, at a point some 12 m. to the south, just along the edge of a cutting in the bed rock of the Acropolis. This cutting has been believed to have been made for the foundations of an altar in front of the Hecatompedon, but the orientation of the one does not agree at all with that of the other, nor for that matter with that of any other nearby remains except the wall A^1 (see PLATE VII). I would suggest, therefore, that the cutting was not made as the bed for any masonry, but marks the corner of the court, where the rock, being somewhat too high, was trimmed away to give a more level grade. The bed rock at Mycenae has been cut away in just this manner along the north side of the court and of the megaron. Even so, the bottom of the cutting here at Athens lies about 50 cm. above the column bases, which presumably were on a level with the court in front of the megaron. But under the circumstances this is not excessive, for at Mycenae the floor of the portico of the megaron, 13.50 m. wide, slopes 20 cm. from one side to the other, as compared with a pitch here in a court, of 50 cm. in 25 m.; and at Tiryns the court slopes 54 cm. in 15 m. If this interpretation of the cutting be correct, then the southern wall of the court lay along its south side, parallel to A^1. The rock, at all times, came right to the surface along this line, so all prehistoric remains would have vanished millenniums ago. The southwestern corner of the court would have lain where the southern boundary meets the line of the façade of the megaron, and though the court so worked out is very irregular in shape,—the appearance is, of course, much worse on the plan than it would be in reality,—yet the megaron is accurately centered on the western side. This last observation, however, should not be given too much weight, since a slight variation in the assumed orientation of the column bases, which are so battered as to make certainty in the matter impossible, might easily swing the façade of the megaron a metre north or south.

The court is about 20 m. wide across the centre, that at Mycenae is about 15.50 m. and the one at Tiryns 20 m. to the front of the colonnades and 25 m. to the back of them. At Tiryns what is supposed to have been an altar stood on axis with the megaron near the opposite wall of the court; at Mycenae there is nothing of the sort. If there ever were one at Athens it probably would have been located about where indicated in Fig. 13.

The megaron of Erechtheus so restored, facing on its court, bears a most striking resemblance in form and size and situation to the eastern cella of the Hecatompedon, before the peristyle was built. Especially is this so if we consider that there may originally have been only four columns within the cella.[1] And in view of what has gone before, this should tend to confirm the restoration. Historically it is quite reasonable that the palace of the prehistoric kings of Athens should have remained practically unchanged in fabric and in function, till kings ceased to exist. The old megaron may have been repaired and somewhat rebuilt along its original lines, its portico may even have disappeared, bringing its face back to the line of the pronaos of the Hecatompedon. But probably when the poros edifice was built in the sixth century it was considered no new departure, but merely a fine new re-creation of the old palace hall, set in the same location, but at a slightly different angle, to make it face squarely on the court. The rooms in the western part may have replaced similar rooms of Mycenaean date, part of the spreading group that formed the original palace complex.[2] Somewhere in this complex there was a shrine. This was probably not the megaron,—for there is no evidence either material or lit-

[1] See above, p. 162, note 1.
[2] Herodotus, (V, 77.) mentions "the megaron which faces west" on the Acropolis at Athens. The expression is unusual; evidently he refers to a large building which is not a "*naos*,"—unless it were a sanctuary of Demeter. The only known large building of that date, which faced west, is the rear portion of the Hecatompedon. Would one not expect this hall to have had a more individual name descriptive of its use, or of its dedication if it were a shrine, or would it not more naturally be described as the western part of the Hecatompedon, if the building as a whole were so called? Or is it possible that the name here used was given in contradistinction to that of the eastern cella, known, perhaps, as "the megaron which faces east" or simply as "the Megaron"?

erary, that Mycenaean megara were ever used as shrines,—but was probably a small low room like the shrines at Cnossus, or like a little room found recently by Mr. Wace at Mycenae, which he thinks may have been a shrine. The megaron was properly the gathering place of the king and his retainers; and it is possible that the Hecatompedon preserved without much change the function as well as the form of the earlier structure. When the Pisistratids ruled regally from the Acropolis, where else could they have lived?

So it seems to me that when Homer wrote, and for some centuries after that, a citizen of Athens might easily imagine his patron goddess visiting the "strong House of Erechtheus." There before him still the palace stood, built by some king in the immemorial past, the great hall of a size his own degenerate era dared not undertake, until at last reborn Athenian skill surpassed that of the earlier days, and the workmen pulled the palace down, a last worn witness of the golden age.

LEICESTER B. HOLLAND

PHILADELPHIA,
1924

American School
of Classical Studies
at Athens

ERECHTHEUM PAPERS

III

THE POST-PERSIAN REVISION

IN 480 B.C. Mardonius captured Athens, and "every part of the citadel"[1] was given to the flames. Just what there was to burn is unknown. The Parthenon had been commenced, the peristyle was partly up, and the whole structure was sheathed with scaffolding. The Hecatompedon, enriched not so very long before by the marble columns and gable sculptures of the Pisistratids, and with all its gay decorations still bright and fresh, lay to the north, facing on an open square. Between these two monuments the central area of the citadel was probably quite open, but venerable clay-roofed structures very likely flanked the north side of the court in front of the Hecatompedon; and in general all the ancient *polis* within the circuit of the thick Pelasgian walls must have been well filled with lesser public structures and with houses dating from the time when this small precinct formed the whole of the city of Athens. Somewhere here, were fortifications built of wood. A little band of desperate souls had trusted these to be the "wooden walls" which Delphi had predicted "safe" and behind them had defied the armies of the Persian king.[2] Perhaps these "wooden walls" were a true stockade, though from the scarcity of heavy timber in the district this seems improbable. More likely they formed a "half-timber" superstructure of brick and wood upon the outer circuit walls of stone, or on some inner terrace walls. At any rate, there must have been enough inflammable material about to make a pretty blaze, and give the Persians some slight satisfaction for the fact that most of the Athenians had eluded them and were safe on Salamis.

Just as we are uncertain what there was on the Acropolis before the fire, so likewise we cannot say how much was left when the fire had died down. All roofs had surely gone, and the blaze of fallen timbers must have calcined the surface of all the lower parts of dressed stone walls, particularly on the inside of the buildings. Herodotus says that some forty years after this he could still see walls there blackened by the Median flames,[3] but these, perhaps, were only the retaining walls of terraces, rough in any case, and thick enough to stand a scorching with impunity. The smaller structures must have

[1] Herodotus, VIII, 53.
[2] *Ibid.* VIII, 51–52. Herodotus says that the entrance to the Acropolis was barricaded with "Θύρῃσί τε καὶ ξύλισι." These were probably roof beams and doors taken from houses on the Acropolis. It is possible that the "wooden walls" were only wooden to this extent.
[3] *Ibid.*. V, 77.

been an almost total loss. The column drums of the Parthenon then in place were so calcined as to be useless except for foundation blocks, or where by trimming off the damaged surfaces they might serve for smaller shafts. The peristyle of the Hecatompedon apparently did not fall, for many unbroken cornice blocks were later built into the north wall of the citadel. These blocks seem also free from damage by fire, and this is natural enough since they would not have been exposed to the direct flames of the burning roof and ceiling of the peristyle even when the woodwork there had fallen. But the column drums were seriously calcined, as they show today, where they lie in the foundations of the north wall. So, although the Persians did not overthrow the peristyle, the Athenians must, themselves, have soon dismantled it for safety's sake.

What was there left of the cella of the Hecatompedon? In cella walls there are few architectural members which can be identified if found re-used in later work, so there is nothing to prove, as do the re-used members of the peristyle and the column drums of the older Parthenon, that the cella of the Hecatompedon did not survive the renovation of the Acropolis. But it is difficult to see how the walls could have escaped being badly calcined, especially on the inner side, where the flames from the fallen timbers of the ceiling and roof must have blazed and glowed close to the soft poros blocks. From general probability one would conclude that when the victors returned from Salamis, nothing was left on the Acropolis but blackened stumps of ruined walls.

Probably what work was done to make these safe for habitation, in the anxious year before Mardonius again swept into Attica, consisted as much in tearing down as it did in building up again. And when a second time Mardonius was forced to leave, "he resolved"—says Herodotus—" to burn Athens, and to cast down and level with the ground whatever remained standing of the walls, temples, and other buildings." [1] How could Herodotus have judged of what Mardonius had intended save by what he knew Mardonius to have done? The cyclopean circuit walls were surely this time largely overthrown, for apparently nothing of them was standing in the late fifth century except the massive section south of the Propylaea. It is hard to believe that, when the Athenians at last were permanently reëstablished in their homes and set to work to reconstruct their shrines and citadel, any walls were standing there that could be used, save only terrace walls and foundations underground.

On the other hand, there are many post-Persian references to an "ἀρχαῖος νεώς." This is identified by Doerpfeld [2] and some others as the cella building of the Hecatompedon. He claims that this

[1] Herodotus. IX, 13.
[2] Doerpfeld's theory of the survival of the Hecatompedon as the "Old Athena Temple" is expounded by him in *Ath. Mitt.* XII, pp. 25 ff., pp. 190 ff.; XV, pp.

"ancient shrine" was not destroyed, but was repaired and stood to the end of classic times. There are also references to an "ὀπισθόδομος" identified by Doerpfeld with the western half of the Hecatompedon. J. W. White [1] advances the theory that the eastern cella was pulled down, but that the "opisthodomos" was restored to serve as a treasury. Neither identification, however, is wholly sure, for many hold that the "ancient shrine" referred to was part of the Erechtheum, and that the "opisthodomos" was the western vestibule or the whole rear section of the Parthenon. The only post-Persian passage that, to my mind, refers with much certainty to the Hecatompedon, is that where Herodotus speaks of "walls blackened by the fires of the Medes, which are over against (or near?) the Megaron that faces to the west." [2] So far as I know, nobody has identified this Mergaron otherwise than as the west cella of the Hecatompedon. But, unfortunately, this mention is unique; there is no other later reference to such a building, at least by that name. I think, therefore, that perhaps, when Herodotus wrote,—some forty years after the fire,— the ruined walls of a part of the Hecatompedon may have been still standing, scorched and crumbling, which shortly after were pulled down and cleared away.[3]

But while the wrath of the Persian king left desolation on the Acropolis, he could not eradicate the sacred sites. The holy olive tree of Athena, so they say, miraculously survived the flames, scorched but not killed; [4] Poseidon's well may have been somewhat dried, but certainly was not destroyed, nor was the mark of the trident that created it erased. The ancient altars may have been overthrown, but to the gods each holy spot was still redolent with centuries of burning flesh and bone. Like cats, the gods sought out their own wrecked *temene* and desolated hearths. So, when the diplomacy of Themistocles and the frantic energy of the citizens

---

420 ff.; XXII, pp. 159 ff. Although Professor Doerpfeld's arguments are in themselves intensely interesting, and the discussion deals with matters closely allied to the subjects of these papers, yet I do not feel that they vitally affect the latter. For Professor Doerpfeld's arguments are based almost wholly on literary evidence, while mine, so far at least, have been based almost wholly on material evidence. The whole subject can readily be reviewed by reference to Frazer, "*Pausanias's Description of Greece*," Vol. II, Appendix, reprinted with slight changes from *J.H.S.* XIII, 1893, pp. 153 ff., or to D'Ooge, *The Acropolis of Athens*, Appendix III.

[1] The Opisthodomos on the Acropolis at Athens, *Harvard Studies*, VI.
[2] Herodotus, V, 77.
[3] There is an inscription (*C.I.A.* I, No. 1, supplemented by *C.I.A.* IV, pp. 3 ff.; Dittenberger, *Syllog. Inscr. Graec.* No. 384) assigned by Kirchhoff and Dittenberger to the first half of the fifth century, which mentions treasures kept "in the *peribolos* south (?) of the old temple of Athena on the Acropolis." "South" is largely restoration, but seems probable. If the "old temple" were on the site of the Erechtheum, then the "enclosure" south of it might very well have been formed by the roofless walls of part of the Hecatompedon, used as a temporary treasury until some more adequate structure should have been built and the unsightly ruin could be removed.
[4] Herodotus, VIII, 55.

had rebuilt the city walls, to assure them from their Spartan allies, Athens turned its attention to the Acropolis with all dispatch, to make the ancient supernatural guardians at home once more, and dress their shrines with even greater glory than before.

Thanks to the thoroughness of the Persian destruction, it was possible to plan the reconstruction on lines more unified and simple than those which had been laid down before, by centuries of slow development. The new circuit wall was built in long straight stretches. The great smooth side of it along the south was the admiration of all Greece. On the north the contours of the rock demanded a more irregular line, but even so, the curves of the old Pelasgian wall were simplified and new areas were enclosed in the Acropolis.

The southern wall is known to be the work of Cimon;[1] the north wall is often attributed to Themistocles, because the use in its foundations of damaged members of the earlier Parthenon and the Hecatompedon seems to agree with the statement of Thucydides[2] that "the base of the fortifications built by Themistocles consists of all sorts of stones,—and many columns from grave monuments and stones wrought for other purposes were built in." But there are marked differences between the wall on the Acropolis and that by the Dipylon gate, which is quite certainly the work of Themistocles; for the latter is built of mixed materials throughout, while in the former re-used stones are limited to those parts below ground,—as seen from the inside,—and to the stretch where the demounted entablature of the Hecatompedon was carefully set up as an enduring token of the barbarous destruction of the Medes. Apparently the rest of the wall was all of fresh-cut poros blocks, neatly drafted along the lower edge on the inner face, and laid with as proper accuracy as the best of poros work can show. The common distinction in period between the north and south walls seems to me, therefore, exaggerated; and as the evidence at present stands, I should credit the Cimonian régime with the general clearing away of the ruins on the Acropolis, and laying out anew, and making fresh again, the ancient *temene* and their sacred shrines.

The most renowned and venerable spots, and those consequently of the first importance, were where the gods, contending for the lordship of the town, had left their marks of prowess, and where the ancient shrine of Athena Polias had stood, housing the heaven-sent ancient wooden *agalma*. The reconstruction of these parts should be the first to be commenced, and possibly work was started

[1] Plutarch (*Cimon*, XIII) says that it was built with the spoils from the battle of the Eurymedon (468 B.C.). Pausanias (I, 28, 3) says, "The whole of the wall which runs round the Acropolis, except the part built by Cimon, son of Miltiades, is said to have been erected by the Pelasgians." In his time, apparently, no part of it was attributed to Themistocles.

[2] Thucydides, I, 93.

here even before the new walls of the Acropolis were built. At any rate, the stretch of wall flanking the "strong house of Erechtheus" on the north seems to be the earliest section of the circuit. For the burned column drums from the older Parthenon are collected here.[1] It is reasonable to use up old materials in foundations first, beginning with the best of these materials, before employing new stone; any other order is unnatural. Where the marble column drum foundations lie the new wall seems to follow very closely the line of the old Cyclopean fortifications, but beyond the easternmost drum the new walls run on east and then southeast, instead of south and then east along the older line.[2] Thus a new corner was included in the Acropolis. And at the west of the column drums the new wall turns sharply northwest and then runs west, while the older wall presumably continued simply west and then turned north. So here, too, the extent of the Acropolis was enlarged. It seems to me quite possible that when the "theatral area" north of the Erechtheum was rebuilt, the stretch of outer wall that bordered it was simultaneously begun,—using the damaged column drums,—and leaving for the moment the old Cyclopean walls at east and west.

But in spite of eagerness for the restoration of the sanctuaries, the work was not begun without due consideration of the plan. An attempt was evidently made, by shifting slightly boundaries here and there, to bring the group of diverse elements into one harmonious scheme. We have seen that the lines of prehistoric masonry in and near the Erechtheum are slightly divergent from one another and from the lines of the classic building,[3] but that the latter agrees exactly with the lines of the cut stone-work of the pre-Erechtheum.[4] This indicates that when the destruction caused by the Persians necessitated a general rebuilding of the Acropolis, a clean sweep was made of the old heterogeneous constructions and a revised plan adopted, which while preserving all the sacred areas, each in its original location and with approximately its original extent, yet by changing their axes slightly, brought them all into one uniform system; and the lines laid down at this time were those followed less than fifty years later by the classic marble structure.

But what was it that determined the new post-Persian axes? Why were those of the Hecatompedon, which so nearly agreed with those of the prehistoric terrace walls, not followed? If the pre-Persian arrangements, as we have seen reason to restore them in the preceding paper, are correct, the reason is not far to seek. To the

---

[1] Here also are steps of Kara stone and of marble from the Parthenon destroyed by the Persians (Hill, *A.J.A.* XVI, 1912, pp. 535 ff).
[2] *Erechtheum Papers II, A.J.A.* XXVIII, pl. VII.
[3] *Erechtheum Papers II, A.J.A.* XXVIII, fig. 12, p. 156.
[4] *Erechtheum Papers I, A.J.A.* XXVIII, p. 21.

north of the Hecatompedon, apparently, lay a "theatral area" bounded on the north, east and south by terraces, (the southern one corresponding roughly to the *temenos* within the east cella of the classic Erechtheum). But since this arrangement had developed from successive periods of building, the surrounding terraces were neither strictly parallel nor mutually at right angles, and the

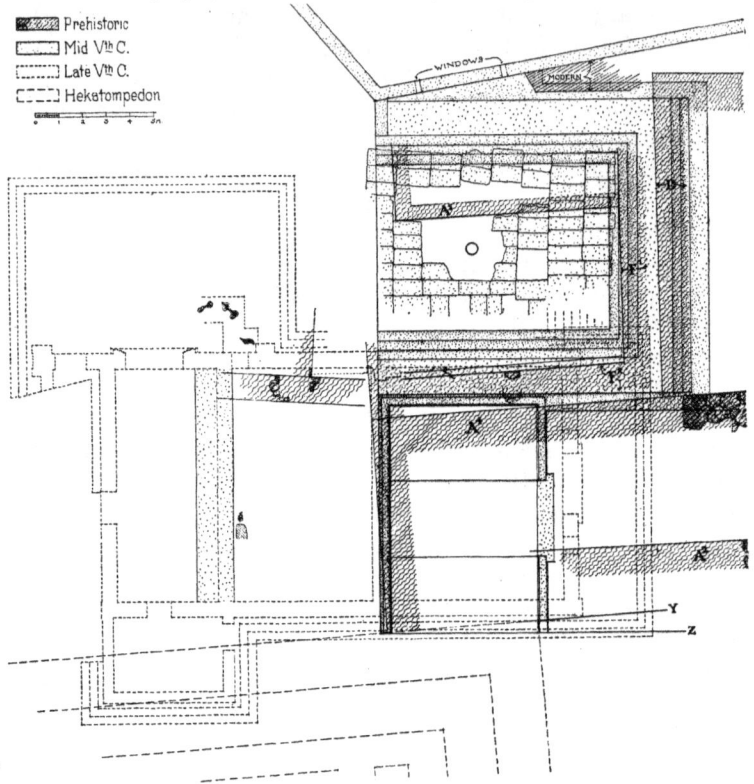

FIGURE 1. SUPERPOSED PLANS OF PRE-ERECHTHEUM CONSTRUCTIONS

southern terrace (F^2) was appreciably longer than that to the north (A^5) (Fig. 1). In the post-Persian revision the trace of the north terrace is clearly marked against the new Cimonian wall.[1] Where the west end of the terrace came, there is an anathyrosis on one of the wall blocks for the abutment of the terrace wall running north and south at the west end of the terrace. This western limit coincides with the point where the circuit wall turns sharply north at the end of the section built on the re-used column drums. We may assume this point to have been determined by the western limit of the pre-Persian "theatral area," or rather by the prehistoric terrace to the

[1] Middleton, *Plans and Drawings of Athenian Buildings*, J.H.S. Suppl. III (1900).

north of that area (A⁵, Fig. 1). The fifth century architect seems to have decided that a line drawn southward from this point should form a continuous western limit for both the new "theatral area" and the terraced *temenos* lying to the south of it, where the east cella of the Erechtheum was later to come. But since, in the old arrangement, this south terrace ran farther west than the northern one, it was necessary to abandon the pre-Persian system of orientation, and run the new western boundary to a point slightly west of the southwest limit of the old terrace, so that the little area clipped from the northwest corner would be compensated for at the southwest. If the older system of lines had been used the terrace would have been reduced a metre and a half. Since it was necessary to do over the whole "theatral area," the other boundaries could easily be shifted by the slight amount needed to conform to the new orientation. And if the orientation of the Hecatompedon was quite disregarded, this may have been because there was no intention of preserving such remains of that building as may have been still standing.

The new eastern boundary of the *temenos* on the south terrace would naturally be parallel to the new western boundary, and we have seen from the cuttings in the foundations of the east wall of the classic Erechtheum that the east boundary lay just within and was exactly parallel to the Erechtheum wall. Therefore we can be reasonably sure that the new western boundary, and in fact all the lines of the revised plan of the "theatral area," were parallel with those of the Erechtheum. Now if the new western boundary be drawn from the sharp angle of the circuit walls southward and parallel to the lines of the Erechtheum, it will be found to fall just in the centre of the east cross wall of that building. Thus, both to the east and to the west, the Cimonian *temenos* on the south terrace agreed with the classic east cella, which merely sheathed the earlier area (Fig. 1).[1]

Of course such a revision required that the west end wall of the prehistoric southern terrace should be torn away, or at least its western face removed, and a new wall be built to the new line on the old foundations. This new wall we may safely assume to have been of poros. And in order that the "theatral area" should lie foursquare with the new west line, it would be necessary to build a new wall for the northern face of the south terrace.

[1] At first sight it would appear that the face of the Cimonian wall should have corresponded with either the east or the west face of the later cross wall, and it is possible that such was actually the case, since a slight variation in what was rather a difficult series of measurements might have shifted my line to the extent of 35 cm. But as Cavvadias's plan (*loc. cit.*) agrees with my own measurements, I believe that the face of the Cimonian wall actually came at the centre of the later wall. In the succeeding paper I shall offer a reason why this should have been the case.

We have seen that from prehistoric times a narrow terrace walk overlooking the "theatral area" ran along the north flank of this south terrace,[1] and we have also seen that at some period this terrace walk was apparently paved with poros.[2] It is reasonable to assume that this poros pavement dates from the Cimonian rebuilding, and as the pavement lay partly, at least, within the Erechtheum, it follows that the Cimonian south terrace must have been somewhat south of the north wall of the Erechtheum. At the same time, it must have been outside, *i.e.* north, of the prehistoric south terrace wall (A^4, Fig. 1). Now it was pointed out in the first paper of this series, that the foundations of the east wall of the classic Erechtheum were laid in an irregular manner. Instead of being begun at one corner and continued across to the other, courses 5 and 6—counting from above—were begun at a point 1.12 m. south of the inner face of the north wall and continued from there toward the south. The gap to the north was filled in when the north wall was laid.[3] If we consider that the face of the Cimonian terrace wall came at this point, it is easy to understand why the later foundations should have been laid as they were. For southward from here the old wall would have to be cut through and the terrace trenched to lay the five lower courses of the new foundations, while to the north the new work could be laid in the open, along with the north wall of the Erechtheum.

Assuming, then, the Cimonian poros terrace wall to have lain parallel to, and 1.12 m. inside the inner face of the north wall of the Erechtheum, we find that at its western end the prehistoric wall of Acropolis limestone (F^2, Fig. 1)[4] which carried the walk at the foot of the old south terrace (A^4) would serve for its foundations. Farther east the new wall would come above the narrow space, less than half a metre wide, between F^2 and A^4, which could easily be filled with rubble to give support. At the eastern end the face of the old wall would have to be somewhat pulled away to make room for the newer work, unless the latter were a mere veneer. For at the point where the old east terrace (D) meets the old south terrace the north face of the new wall would lie only 20 cm. to the north of the latter.

Now, though there is nothing to indicate that the ancient south terrace, between the "theatral area" and the royal Megaron or later Hecatompedon, served as a sacred *temenos* in Mycenaean or pre-Persian times, it is evident that it did so in the post-Persian revision, for the cuttings on the inside of the south foundations of the Erechtheum show that it was enclosed on the east, with a long

[1] *Erechtheum Papers* II, *A.J.A.* XXVIII, p. 158.
[2] *Erechtheum Papers* I, *A.J.A.* XXVIII, pp. 11–12.
[3] *Erechtheum Papers* I, *A.J.A.* XXVIII, pp. 17–18 and pl. I, C.
[4] *Erechtheum Papers* II, *A.J.A.* XXVIII, fig. 12, p. 156.

sill or step giving access to it from that side. Undoubtedly it bore the same dedication and served much the same purpose as the east cella of the Erechtheum which replaced it, and it is altogether probable that the special sanctity of the area long antedated the Persian destruction.

On the east and west the boundaries of the *temenos* lie just within those of the east cella; on the north the outer face of the boundary wall would be from 1.10 m. to 1.20 m. south of the inner face of the Erechtheum wall. Where did the southern boundary lie? The old Mycenaean terrace wall (A^2) must have been abandoned, for the new entrance sill ran south of that line, but some other terrace wall must have been built in its place to effect the transition between the level in front of the Hecatompedon and that in front of the "east cella" *temenos*, about a metre and a half below. Cavvadias[1] shows no trace of any such wall, though possibly a reëxcavation of the region might give some indication of its position. There is no way of knowing whether it was built before or after the Persian destruction, though the latter seems to me the more probable. If it were pre-Persian it would probably have been parallel to the lines of the Hecatompedon and almost parallel to A^2 (as at Y, Fig. 1), but if it were post-Persian its line would probably be parallel to those of the new *temenos* and "theatral area,"—and, of course, the subsequent Erechtheum. In any case, it seems unlikely that the *Kara* stone foundations of the peristyle of the Hecatompedon would be left unchanged, to flank the south side of the "east cella" *temenos* on a line bias to the other three sides. More probably it would be built out with poros to a line, on the new system, running west from the northwest angle of the peristyle foundations, or else, since the perisytle itself was unquestionably removed after the fire, it may be that the foundations were dressed back to a line at right angles to the west wall of the *temenos*, drawn from the point where that wall met the peristyle, and that the new terrace wall continued the same line out to the east (as at Z, Fig. 1). This second arrangement would bring the southern limit of the *temenos* about 3.10 m. south of the south end of the entrance sill. (A variation of ten centimetres or so from this figure is quite possible, since the point of intersection of the hidden foundations of the Hecatompedon with the non-existent west wall of the *temenos* is difficult to locate exactly.) If the sill ran as far north as the point marked m^3, as seems most likely, its northern end would lie about 3.42 m. to the south of the presumed line of the outer face of the terrace wall bounding the *temenos* on the north.[2] Upon this wall there must have been a parapet; if the inner face of the parapet came 0.32 m. south of the

---

[1] Cavvadias und Kawerau, *Ausgrabung der Akropolis*, pl. Γ.
[2] *Erechtheum Papers* I, A.J.A. XXVIII pl. I, C.

outer face of the supporting terrace wall, the sill would then be exactly centred on the interior of the *temenos*. A symmetrical arrangement of this sort is inherently probable, since the Cimonian rebuilding started with a practically clear field and apparently endeavored to lay out the ancient sanctuaries in a coördinated monumental scheme. The interior width of the *temenos* so planned is 9.90 m., just 5 cm. more than the interior width of its successor, the east cella of the Erechtheum: the depth from east to west would be 6.30 m. as opposed to 7.30 m. in the later building. The prehistoric terrace was about 6.10 m. from north to south, including the width of the parapet, and if the east boundary continued the front line of the Hecatompedon, it was 6.30 m. from east to west, including parapets at both ends. Each alteration increased the area of the sanctuary very slightly.

The parapets on the north and west sides of the Cimonian *temenos* would naturally be similar to that along the east side, and the cuttings in the foundations of the southeast corner of the Erechtheum give us some idea as to its nature there.[1] Apparently it consisted of slabs, probably of marble, set on edge; the total distance from the outer face of the supporting wall to the inner face of the upright slabs being somewhat less than 0.323 m. (Fig. 2). This agrees admirably with the hypothetical thickness assumed for the parapet along the north side of the *temenos*. The top of the slabs was very likely level with the stylobate of the Hecatompedon; the bottom rested on a course flush with the entrance sill, or more probably on a base 0.295 m. thick set upon that course. The top of the base would be at the level of the top of the orthostates of the later Erechtheum.

The ground level to the east of the *temenos* must have been at least a few centimetres below the top of the entrance sill: or if this were a step instead of a flush sill, the grade would come at the top of a euthynteria about 30 cm. below. The level of the terrace to the north of the "theatral area," as marked against the inside of the Acropolis wall, lay at exactly the level of the top of the orthostates of the north wall of the Erechtheum. We should expect the levels of the two terraces flanking the "theatral area" to be the same, for while that of the *temenos* to the south might have been predetermined by some special factor, there is no apparent reason why that to the north could not have been made to match it. If we assume, then, the level within the *temenos* to have been one step higher than the top of the sill, the arrangement at the entrance would have been somewhat as shown in A or C (Fig. 3). The depth of the cutting in the foundations of the Erechtheum is suitable for a step (30 cm., see Fig. 2), which would naturally be about

[1] *Erechtheum Papers* I, *A.J.A.* XXVIII, pp. 21–22.

as high as it was wide; but if the grade to the east came 30 cm. below the top of the cutting, the foundation course or euthynteria, which projected as far as the face of the step, would have been

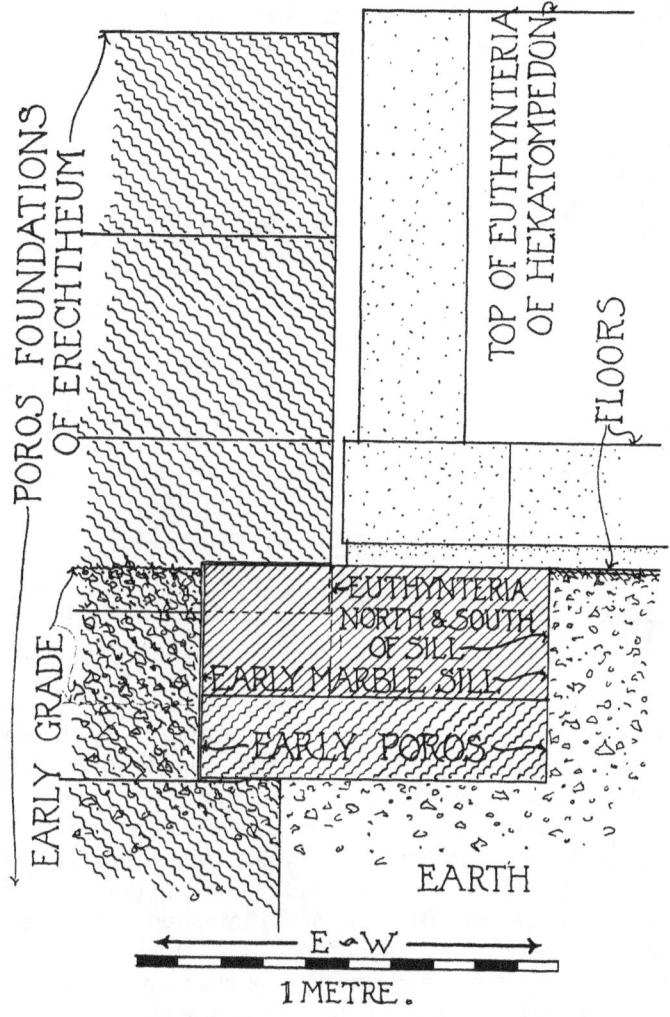

FIGURE 2. SECTION THROUGH ENTRANCE TO "EAST CELLA" TEMENOS SHOWING RELATION OF EARLIER CONSTRUCTION TO FOUNDATION OF EAST WALL OF ERECHTHEUM (cf. *Erechtheum Papers I*, Pl. I, D)

exposed all across the front of the *temenos* (A, Fig. 3). On the other hand, the arrangement shown in C (Fig. 3) is anomalous and improbable; for while a sill flush with the grade level at both sides is normal enough—there is such a one in the Cimonian remains in the Pandroseum, to be considered in a subsequent paper—there is no object in a flush sill projecting from beneath a step.

It is also possible that the *temenos* was not of a uniform level, but was flush with the sill or step in the centre and a step higher at the north and south sides; and the likelihood of such an arrangement is supported by the probable existence of a similar arrangement in the east cella of the Erechtheum which succeeded it. In

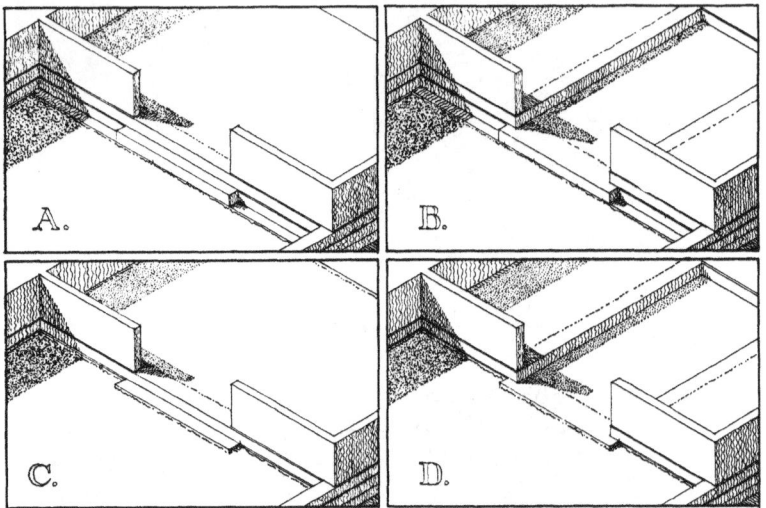

FIGURE 3. POSSIBLE ARRANGEMENTS OF "EAST CELLA" TEMENOS

the southeast corner of the classic building there projects inward a broken piece of the marble course which outside forms the lower torus and scotia of the moulded base around the building.[1] This indicates that here, at least, the floor level was at the top of this course. But we should naturally expect this to be also the level of the top of the sill of the door from the east porch, for it marks the line of division between base and orthostate, and is the level of the sill leading into the Porch of the Maidens. In classic doorways of the fifth century it was the rule for the floor within a doorway to be at the same level as that of the porch without. This is the case with the Parthenon and with the north door to the Erechtheum as originally planned, though in the latter case the inner floor actually came 0.105 m. higher than at first intended, reducing the height of the sill on the inside to 0.317 m. In the Porch of the Maidens the sill is the full height of the base course above the floor inside. Stevens, in his restoration of the east doorway,[2] brings the sill still

[1] *Erechtheum Papers* I, A.J.A. XXVIII, pl. I, C and D.
[2] A.J.A. X, pp. 47 ff.

higher, up to the top of the upper torus above the base course cut on the outer side of the orthostates. This would necessitate cutting away the orthostates to fit over the ends of the sill, and even so would only bring the sill 10 cm. above the floor level indicated in the southeast corner, which Stevens assumes for the whole cella. It seems to me much more probable that the sill came only to the top of the base course, and that the floor in the central part of the east cella was on a level with that of the east porch; the floor along the north and south sides of the cella being raised a low step above it, as in the great cella of the Parthenon. The width of the east door and its trim, as fixed with practical certainty by Stevens's brilliant restoration, is such that the length of the sill would be just one third of the total width of the interior of the east cella. This suggests that the three divisions of the floor were of equal width, with a step at either end of the sill running at right angles to it, and equal to it in height.

If we apply this same triple division to the Cimonian *temenos* on the site of the east cella, we find that it works out surprisingly well. The Cimonian sill was 3.70 m. long; the inside width of the *temenos* was approximately 9.90 m., which divided by three gives 3.30 m. for each section. This would very likely correspond to the width of the entrance to the *temenos*, the parapet overlapping the sill by 0.20 m. at each end. The appearance of the entrance would then have been as in B or D (Fig. 3).

The "theatral area" to the north was paved with slabs of marble when the classic Erechtheum was built. These were set on an under layer of large poros blocks. The marble pavement is now wholly gone, save where a few pieces of it are engaged under the north wall of the Erechtheum and the east steps of the north porch, but the poros layer seems intact, except for two holes near the centre of the area. From one of these some fifteen blocks have been removed; from the other, two blocks are gone. On the east, the poros blocks run clear up to the remains of the Mycenaean wall F^1 (Fig. 1).[1] But the wide flight of marble steps, built with the Erechtheum, which led from the "theatral area" to the upper level at the east, commenced at a point nearly three metres west of the eastern edge of the poros blocks. This proves, I think, beyond doubt, that the marble and poros constructions are not contemporary. For while the poros blocks might possibly have been laid as an exceptionally heavy foundation for the marble pavement, there is no reason at all why the layer should have been extended beneath the marble steps. At the west the poros pavement stops against two cisterns of mediaeval construction. It is possible that one or two more rows of poros blocks were removed when these were built, but it is

[1] *Erechtheum Papers* II, *A.J.A.* XXVIII, pl. VII.

quite as likely that this spot was chosen for them because there was no pavement here. At the north the pavement ends some 2.00 m. to 2.50 m. south of the nearest point in the Acropolis wall. It is of course possible that it once continued all the way to the wall, but as it stops in a definite though very irregular line it is probable that it never extended any farther than at present. The poros blocks vary considerably in shape and size, averaging 0.40 m. to 0.55 m. in depth, 0.60 m. to 0.70 m. in width, and 1.20 m. to 1.40 m. in length. Their surfaces are rough and they are irregularly laid; at one time they must have been covered with a coat of stucco to give a proper finish to the top.[1] The size of the blocks is much greater than is customary or reasonable for a pavement, and the sides and ends are so very rough,—though they have not been greatly exposed to the weather,—the angles so rounded and the shapes so irregular that the suspicion is unavoidable that they originally belonged to some pre-Persian construction and, having been damaged by the fire, were roughly redressed to serve as the basis of a stucco pavement here. Directly beneath them, in places, is a layer of five to ten centimetres of poros chips. These have become so disintegrated by moisture and have so coalesced with the under surface of the blocks above, that it is sometimes impossible to tell just where the division originally came. This under layer is probably the calcined surface which was removed when the blocks were redressed.

If these poros pavement blocks formed part of a wall at the time of the fire, the top and bottom surfaces would probably not have been much damaged, while the outer and inner surfaces might need to be cut away to a considerable extent. In accordance with normal fifth-century proportions for wall blocks, they might have originally been somewhere around 0.60–0.70 m. high, by 0.80–0.90 m. wide, by 1.60–1.80 m. long, though of course the length in an early wall may not have been uniform. To judge from the pre-Persian architectural remains found on the Acropolis,[2] there was only one building large enough to have used *plinthoi* of anything like this size; and that was the Hecatompedon. The narrowest of the rough foundation walls for that building are 1.35 m. wide; the wall sill would naturally have been narrower than this, there may have been a projecting course at the base of the orthostates, and these in turn would project a little beyond the wall above; so that an orthostate course about 0.95 m. thick surmounted by a wall of about 0.85 m. is altogether reasonable.[3] The old triglyphs of the cella wall were 1.82 m. on

---

[1] *Erechtheum Papers* II, *A.J.A.* XXVIII, figs. 4–7, pp. 148–51.

[2] Wiegand, *Poros Architektur der Akropolis*.

[3] The cella walls of the Heraeum at Olympia, across the orthostates, are 1.18 m. wide, while the foundations are from 1.80 m. to 2.10 m. wide. The orthostates of the temple of Zeus, there, are 1.32 m. wide, and the wall sill beneath them is 1.63 m. (Curtius-Adler, *Olympia*, Vol. I).

centres; this may have been the length of the wall blocks also. It is of course possible that these *plinthoi* never belonged to any building at all, but came from some fortification or terrace wall, but it seems much more probable that up to the period of the Persian wars, everything of the latter sort on the Acropolis was built of Acropolis limestone or Kara stone, rather than of squared poros masonry. And the Hecatompedon was so near to the "theatral area" that it would be very natural to use the debris of the ruined building in this place.

In the pre-Persian arrangement of the "theatral area" a terrace walk, slightly over a metre and a half wide, presumably ran along the southern and eastern sides, at the foot of the main flanking terraces. There is evidence to show that when the Erectheum was being built a similar terrace walk, of poros, lay just within, and by careful underpinning was incorporated in the new construction.[1] This poros terrace would seem to be the Cimonian revision of the pre-Persian one. It lay along the new terrace wall of the "east cella" *temenos* with its northern edge at a line somewhat north of the inner face of the later Erechtheum wall. This gives a minimum width of 1.10 m.: probably it was nearly as wide as the 1.50 m. terrace which preceded it. Its upper surface could not have been much below the level of the classic floor in the west cella of the Erechtheum, since the bottoms of the slabs which formed the terrace floor were in places less than 40 cm. below that level,[2] and poros slabs would hardly have been cut much less than 40 cm. thick. Obviously these were not removed when the classic building was erected, or they would not have been so elaborately underpinned; yet it would certainly seem easier to have done so than to have dressed them down enough (20 cm. or so) to have laid a new floor on top of them. Therefore, I believe that the original level of the terrace walk was the same as that of the classic floor, and that while in the east cella it was buried when the Erechtheum was built, yet its continuation in the west cella actually served as the classic floor, for a strip along the wall at least.

Now if the foundations of the east wall of the Erechtheum be examined,[3] it will be seen that not only do courses 5 and 6 (counting from above) break at the point where the face of the north wall of the "east cella" *temenos* is presumed to have come, but that courses 7 and 8 do not carry through, at a uniform height, for their full length. The bed of course 6 is continuous from end to end, but south of the line of the *temenos* wall, the course is 48 cm. high, while to the north it is only 38 cm.; the top coming to the probable floor level of the terrace walk. Now just below this, at the north end, course 7 is also 38 cm. high, though for all the rest of its length it is 44.7 cm. And the

---

[1] *Erechtheum Papers* I, *A.J.A.* XXVIII, pp. 7–12.
[2] *Erechtheum Papers* I, *A.J.A.* XXVIII, pl. I, A.
[3] *Erechtheum Papers* I, *A.J.A.* XXVIII, pl. I, C.

total distance from the top of the terrace walk down to the level of the poros pavement of the "theatral area," is 1.543 m., *i. e.* almost exactly four times 38.8 cm. This suggests immediately, that the north face of the terrace walk was built in four courses, each 38–38.8 cm. high, with which the northern end of the east foundation courses of the Erechtheum were aligned.

The southernmost of the poros blocks in the pavement of the "theatral area" are oriented north and south, while all the other blocks

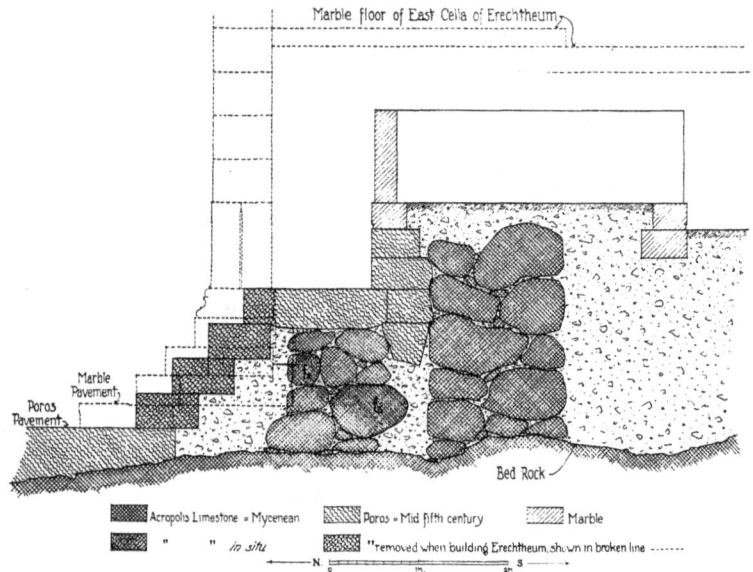

FIGURE 4. SECTION THROUGH NORTH SIDE OF "EAST CELLA" TEMENOS. (*Cf. Erechtheum Papers I, Pl. I, B and C.*)

run east and west. It looks as if the order of laying had been: first the north-south blocks as a row of headers along the southern limit of the area; then a row of headers along the eastern limit,—these of course running east and west,— then successive rows from east to west, the blocks in each row being laid from south to north, starting against the ends of the southern row of headers. If this be correct, the southern boundary of the "theatral area" must have been at the south end of the southern row of poros blocks. Unless these are inordinately long they cannot extend far south of the face of the lowest step of the Erechtheum, and yet they probably extended a little beneath the contemporary Cimonian structure. But if the four courses upholding the terrace walk formed a vertical wall on the line of the lowest step of the Erechtheum, the walk would be 2. 65 m. wide; whereas the preceding one was only about 1.50 m. wide, and in the succeeding structure, only the three marble steps remained as a reminiscence of its existence. It seems unlikely, also, that a terrace wall on that line would have affected the coursing of the east foundations of the Erechtheum so far to the south. Therefore, I think it much more probable that the four courses of the terrace formed four steps, each about 38 cm. high. In Figure 4 I have assumed a width of 40 cm. for each step, which, with the face of the lowest step on the line of the face of the later marble step, gives a terrace walk at the top 1.44 m. wide. The north edge of this terrace walk, for a width of

FIGURE 5. OUTER FACE OF THE EAST FOUNDATIONS OF THE ERECHTHEUM IN 1886

35 cm., and the three lower steps, would have been removed when the classic Erechtheum was built.

At the west end of the stretch within the later east cella, the old Acropolis limestone wall would support only the southern half of the poros slabs paving the terrace walk; hence there would be a real reason here for underpinning when the Cimonian steps were removed and the classic fifth century work begun.

In the years following 1885, while the excavations of the Acropolis were in progress, the German Institute in Athens took photographs of regions then laid bare but which have since been covered up again. One such photograph (Fig. 5)[1] shows the outer face of the east foundations of the Erechtheum. Unfortunately the plate has deteriorated very much in the course of time, and details which are fairly

[1] I am indebted to the kindness of the German Institute for permission to publish this photograph for the first time. Extensive retouching has been necessary to make reproduction possible. This has been done with the greatest care, and constant comparison with an early print and with another photograph taken from a slightly different angle, has, I think, assured against misrepresentation of the evidence.

clear on an old print in the archives of the Institute, have become quite indistinct. It can be seen, however, that at the bottom the foundations project well east of the euthynteria of the superstructure. The prehistoric wall A^4 is seen to run close against these foundations, indicating that it was cut through when the poros work was laid. Just to the north of the north face of A^4 there is a break in the coursing of the foundations. This break corresponds with the break noted on the inside of the foundation wall, which was taken as an indication of the position of the face of the north wall of the "east cella" *temenos*. Three courses up from the ground, to the north of this break, is a large and thin horizontal poros block, the position and level of which exactly agree with that of the hypothetical poros slabs paving the south terrace walk. Above this block the foundations shown in the photograph are in large part mediaeval or modern. It would seem as if when the southern part of the classic foundations had been laid as far as the Cimonian terrace wall, the remaining northeast corner was then filled in with very inferior material, which has since disintegrated; or that it was thought unnecessary to carry the foundations here solidly to the rock. And as a matter of fact, with the great flight of marble steps, which led up from the "theatral area," serving as a buttress and retaining wall to the north, very light foundations for the porch would have been adequate, though they would have indicated a marked decline from the solid construction of earlier work.

A reëxcavation of the foundations of the Erechtheum would probably bring to light many very interesting details, and would certainly confirm or refute many of the theories advanced in these papers, but in default of that, the faded photograph seems to me to show quite definitely that a terrace walk paved with poros slabs, much as has been deduced from other evidence, once flanked the "theatral area"; and that probably part of the pavement is still *in situ*, buried now underground.

The cuttings on the tops of the blocks inserted when the classic Erechtheum was built, to support the north ends of the pavement slabs of the older terrace walk, show the latter to have had irregular and slightly convex under surfaces. This points to their having been re-used blocks, damaged by fire, like the pavement blocks of the "theatral area." Their thickness as finished, seems to have varied from 0.325 m. to nearly 0.45 m.; their width, from east to west, as indicated by the cuttings of the underpinning, ranged from 0.80 m. to about 1.25 m., and their length has been assumed to be about 1.44 m. If the pavement blocks of the "theatral area" came from a wall about 0.85 m. wide, with courses roughly 0.65 m. high and blocks somewhere around 1.70 m. long, then the slabs of the terrace walk might very well have been broken orthostates from the same wall,—

originally two wall courses (1.30 m.) high, by a little over half the wall-thickness (0.425 m.) wide, and with the same length as the *plinthoi* (1.70 m.),—the under surfaces, as re-used, being those exposed to the fire in their original situation.

North of the "theatral area" a terrace, as has been noted before, of the height assumed for the "east cella" *temenos*, covered the lower part of the inner face of the Cimonian Acropolis wall. If the poros pavement of the "theatral area" originally stopped where it now does, this northern terrace must have extended far enough south to cover the irregular edge of the northern row of pavement blocks (Fig. 1). Yet it could not reasonably have reached far enough south to have covered the southern edge of any of them, for if in any case a block had been entirely covered, that block would have been unnecessary. Thus the southern limit of the northern terrace is located within a zone 30 cm. wide,—always assuming that the poros pavement is of its original extent. The northern terrace might have been a simple high level, held up by a sheer wall at its southern edge, but in view of the general character of the post-Persian revision, it seems much more likely that the northern terrace was treated like that to the south of the "theatral area," with a terrace walk and four steps at its foot. And if a line for the northern terrace be drawn to the east from the point of the angle of the Acropolis wall which marks the western limit of the "theatral area," it will be found that a terrace walk and four steps, of the same width as that determined for those along the southern terrace, will just reach to the proper zone on the northern row of blocks of the poros pavement (Fig. 1).

An argument in support of this arrangement is offered by two narrow slit windows in the Acropolis wall, at the points shown on Figure 1.[1] These date, beyond any question, from the original post-Persian building of the wall, and are therefore contemporary with the northern terrace. But their sills are only 0.55 m. and their heads only 1.10 m. above the level indicated for that terrace. On the other hand, the sills are 3.06 m. above the poros pavement of the "theatral area." In the one case they are too low, in the other too high to have been of any use. But with a terrace walk at the level of that to the south of the "theatral area," the sills of the windows would come 1.52 m. above the feet of a watcher standing there, and the heads 0.55 m. higher. And with the northern terrace as shown in Figures 1 and 6, the hypothetical guardian would stand only 0.35 m. away from one window and 1.00 m. away from the other. He could easily lean forward till his face came close against the openings.

At the east of the "theatral area" there was probably a similar arrangement also, for the east ends of the eastern blocks of the

[1] See Middleton, *loc. cit.*

poros pavement must have been covered, and yet the southern terrace walk, and consequently that at the east, too, must have extended east as far as the slab shown *in situ* in Figure 5, *i. e.* beyond the western face of the prehistoric terrace wall D. I am inclined to doubt that at the east the terrace rose in a straight wall from the terrace walk, as it did on the south and north, for in such case foundations should have been carried down to bedrock, and there should be some trace of them in Figure 5 or on the plans of Cavvadias.[1] I think it more likely that steps, not requiring deep foundations, led from the walk to the upper level (Fig. 6). There would thus be a flight, broken at mid-height, all across the east end

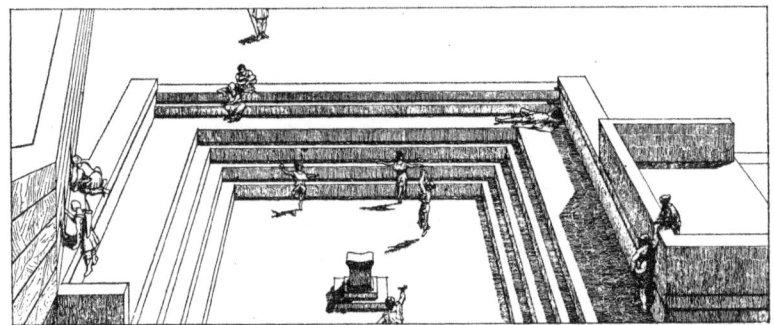

FIGURE 6. AREA NORTH OF ERECHTHEUM IN THE MIDDLE OF THE FIFTH CENTURY

of the "theatral area," which would prepare the way naturally for the continuous flight of marble steps built a half century later.

The level of the northern terrace, where its trace is visible at its west end, has been assumed for that of the "east cella" *temenos* directly across from it, but the level to the east of the *temenos* was certainly one or two steps lower. There does not seem to be any logical place in the northern or eastern terrace for a step down to this latter level, and therefore I have shown in Figure 1 the course on which the parapet of the *temenos* rests, running continuously along the northern, eastern and southern terraces. If the level east of the *temenos* were as shown in A and B (Fig. 2), there would then be a wall along it two courses high, which is rather too little for a parapet and rather too much for a simple coping. I therefore think the grade shown in C and D more probable; for a coping a single course high forms a very reasonable edge for a low terrace. At the east this coping may have continued across the top of the steps, as shown in Figure 1, or to avoid going up an unnecessary step and then down again, it may have stopped at the ends of the flight, as shown in Figure 5.

[1] *Loc. cit.*

The "theatral area" thus laid out has a length from east to west of approximately 9.75 m. and a width of 7.00 m., while its pre-Persian forerunner had a length of 9.35–10.75 m. and a width of about 6.65 m. As in the case of the "east cella" *temenos*, the extent of the sacred area remains almost constant, the change consisting of a re-orientation and a very slight increase in size.

The absence of a considerable number of poros blocks from the centre of the poros pavement of the "theatral area," requires some explanation. These blocks were not of a size or condition to have been of much use to mediaeval builders, and if they had been wanted for such use, they would probably not have been taken from the centre of the area, whence they would be much more difficult to extract than from around the edge. Moreover, five of them were not removed as a whole, but were broken across and only in part taken out. It seems clear from this, that the aim of the mediaeval workmen was not primarily to abstract blocks, but rather to make a hole in the pavement. And to one familiar with mediaeval, and in fact modern, practices in Greece, their ulterior object is evident,— they were digging for buried treasure! In the same way and for a similar reason blocks were removed from the floor of the *tholos* in the "Marmaria" at Delphi. The hole in the "theatral area" was apparently started by cutting through the blocks in a rough circle, the centre of which is marked on Figure 1 by a small ring. Needless to say, the seekers found no treasure, but at the north of their hole they must have uncovered the prehistoric wall A[5]. Led on by this mysterious underground structure, they evidently removed a good many more blocks to the north. In time the search was abandoned as fruitless, and the hole filled up again: thus the old wall was preserved for the discussions of modern archaeologists. But why did the diggers suspect that a treasure lay hidden beneath the poros blocks at the point marked with a ring on Figure 1. It must be that just at that spot there was something peculiar in the material or in the manner of laying of the pavement of the "theatral area," which was exposed when the marble slabs of the later pavement were taken away to serve in Byzantine or Turkish dwellings. Now it can be seen on Figure 1 that the ring comes exactly on the axis of the "theatral area," as laid out there. I do not think that this can be mere coincidence, but regard it rather as good evidence that the north and south limits of the Cimonian "theatral area" were approximately where I have located them; and the fact that the distance from this south limit to the terrace wall of the "east cella" *temenos*, as indicated by the classic foundations of the Erechtheum, agrees so perfectly with the distance from the north limit to the reëntrant angle of the Acropolis wall, seems to me to confirm the hypothesis of similar terrace walks along the north and south. The vanished construction that hinted at buried treasure, in the middle ages, must have been the base of a dedicatory monument, or an altar, or the pedestal of a statue, which stood on the axis of the "theatral area" (Fig. 6) and about which the fifth century ceremonies there were centred. The two blocks missing from the hole to the southeast of the main hole in the poros pavement, were shallow blocks resting on bedrock, which had been dressed away here to receive them when they were laid. It is probable that they have merely disintegrated and were never intentionally removed.

There is little to say about the Cimonian constructions to the west of the "theatral area." The poros blocks of the pavement extend somewhat beyond the theoretical western limit of the area. But this is easily accounted for by the fact that the rows of re-used blocks were laid from east to west, taking them as they came without dressing them down to a predetermined size. And when the last row was laid it was probably found easier to let it project beyond the proper limit than to cut off the ends of the blocks. The stucco coating above would serve to true up the area.

The level of the southern terrace walk undoubtedly continued past the west line of the "theatral area" and the "east cella" *temenos*. Probably it gave the level for the area within the east part of the west cella of the later Erechtheum. And I think it probable that the four steps leading up to this terrace walk also continued west until they met the construction—whatever that may have been—surrounding the mysterious god-made holes in the Acropolis rock;[1] but here there is no material evidence at all.

The heavy poros foundations of the west cross wall of the Erechtheum may also be, in part, of Cimonian workmanship. They certainly do not belong with the classic foundations of the exterior walls, for they are noticeably inferior to the latter in technique. Furthermore, as Elderkin has pointed out,[2] the Acropolis rock has been carefully cut to provide level beds for the foundations of the exterior walls, but not for the cross wall foundations, nor do the courses of the latter bond in with the former at either end. It is Elderkin's opinion that the foundations of the cross wall are entirely of Roman date. Mr. Stevens, on the other hand, from a careful examination of the earth between the stones, has come to the conclusion that the two upper courses are Roman, but that the two lower ones are Greek. My own opinion is that Stevens is correct in considering the lower courses earlier than the upper ones, but that Elderkin is correct also in holding that they were not built along with the late fifth-century Erechtheum. The evidence seems to me to indicate, in fact, that they were built before, rather than after the

---

[1] *Erechtheum Papers* II, *A.J.A.* XXVIII, pp. 159–160.
[2] *Problems in Periclean Buildings*, p. 24.

classic work. For at the north end of the cross wall (Fig. 7), the corner of one of the poros blocks seems clearly to have been cut into, in order to lay the marble foundations of the north wall against and upon it. And since there is such ample evidence of a general reconstruction in poros after the Persian fire, on the exact orientation of this wall, and since the Cimonian restorations,—in the remains of the old gate on the site of the Propylaea as well as in the pre-Erech-

FIGURE 7. ABUTMENT OF WEST CROSS WALL AGAINST JAMB OF DOOR TO CRYPT

theum,—show many signs of hasty or careless workmanship, I see no reason to doubt that here also we have work of the post-Persian revision.[1] There is nothing to indicate what part this wall played in the general scheme, but its integral solidity and freedom from cuttings for contact with other stones indicates that no prehistoric

[1] The blocks of the two lower courses of this west cross-wall foundation are of approximately the same size as the poros blocks of the "theatral area." They are .43−.50m. ×.50−.62m. ×1.20−1.22m. but do not differ greatly from the blocks of the foundation of the north wall of the Erechtheum which were cut to multiples of the Attic foot and are approximately .492m. ×.656m. ×1.31m.

masonry preceded it there. The stone marked "g"[1] may perhaps belong to a construction farther east, which was replaced by the Cimonian cross wall; but further material evidence in this region is altogether lacking.

Still farther west[2] there are bits of post-Persian construction at the entrance from the north porch into the Pandroseum, and the poros foundations and rock cuttings for the foundations of the west part of the Pandroseum wall probably date from the same period. These will be further considered in a later paper. Lastly, there is a line of poros foundations running from the Acropolis wall, at a point still farther west, in a south-easterly direction toward the northwest corner of the Pandroseum.[3] The inside of the Acropolis wall[4] shows that to the east of these foundations the grade was probably the same as that of the "theatral area," while to the west it was over two metres lower. Probably there was a retaining wall here which, from the fifth century on, formed the western boundary of that whole congeries of ancient sanctuaries known to the Athenians as "the Erechtheum."

IV

"The Building Called the Erechtheum"

In periods of rapid architectural development the newest work very quickly becomes the oldest. The ancient shrines of Erechtheus and related deities, having been first in the Athenian effort to reëmbellish the Acropolis, were speedily surpassed by greater architectural glories. Eagerness and a ready supply of secondhand materials had no sooner clothed these shrines with poros, plaster coated and picked out with marble trimmings, than the Parthenon, drawing on the common purse of the Delian league, blossomed forth in finest marble of Pentelicon, with only a few old blocks, and those of marble too, reworked for the new construction. And hardly was that done, when the gates of the Acropolis, which Cimon had restored in plastered poros, trimmed with marble, were replaced by the great new Propylaea built, all of new material, with an architectural freedom and new daring,—as in the solid marble roof of the central hall,—which in its way surpassed the Parthenon. Thus, in less than fifty years the newest work on the Acropolis became the oldest there, and the "Temple" with its adjacent areas, though still supreme in sanctity, came to present an unbecoming air of poverty and neglect. So, as at the Propylaea, the Athenians set to work to replace the poros work

---

[1] Fig. 1, cf. *Erechtheum Papers* I, *A.J.A.* XXVIII, p. 16.
[2] *Erechtheum Papers* I, *A.J.A.* XXVIII, figs. 7 and 8, p. 10.
[3] *Erechtheum Papers* II, *A.J.A.* XXVIII, pl. VII.
[4] Cavvadias, *op. cit.* figs. 1, 2 and pl. K.

of Cimon with marble work of Pericles. The outcome was the present building "called the Erechtheum." [1]

In preceding papers I have given more or less elaborate restorations of earlier structures on this site. These lay no claim to certainty in the detailed arrangements shown,—though no detail has been put down without some reason to sustain it,—but the general outline of the history of the building cannot, I think, be doubted: i.e., that from prehistoric times the site was marked with sacred areas; that these persisted with little change down to the time of the Persian conflagration; that they were then rebuilt with practically the same locations and sizes as before, but with a slightly shifted and now homogeneous orientation; and that the last rebuilding, in the second half of the fifth century, still paid scrupulous respect to the ancient areas and followed exactly the orientation of the Cimonian work. Apart from the substitution of marble for poros, the chief achievement of the Periclean building was the bringing beneath a single simple roof areas which had theretofore been variously roofed or left quite open to the sky.

If the restoration which I have given for the poros period be approximately correct, it is easy to see how the Erechtheum came to be designed as it was. (Fig. 1, shown in broken lines.) We have found no evidence as to what lay in the area of the western cella, nor have we examined as yet the region west of the Erechtheum, but there is patent proof that to the westward lay an enclosure walled on the north and west, and probably with an east wall also, not far from the later west wall of the Erechtheum. The poros foundations of the west cross-wall, which seem to be pre-Periclean,[2] indicate that between them and the east cross-wall there probably lay another sacred area, walled in, presumably, on the west cross-wall foundations. The space between this enclosure and the one to the west of the Erechtheum may also have been a sacred *temenos*, but if the stairs in the Porch of the Maidens are the successors of a prehistoric stairway at approximately the same point,—and this seems to me almost certain in view of the continuity in function shown elsewhere in the temple area,—then the region between them and the North Porch must always have served as an approach, a sort of forecourt corridor, giving access to sacred *temene* on the right hand and the left and to the stairway at the end.

This corridor-court the architect evidently sought to treat symmetrically. On the east it was to be flanked by a wall set on the midline of the foundations already there (one Attic foot east of where the

---

[1] The modern name for the ruin is sponsored by Pausanias, who says, in the course of his tour of the Acropolis (I, 26, 5), "There is also a building called the Erechtheum." The only other occurrence of this name in classic writings is in the life of Lycurgus, by the pseudo-Plutarch, p. 843e.
[2] See above, pp. 423–424.

wall was actually built), the stairs at the south would determine the axis of the hall, and the west side would be closed by the west wall of the Erechtheum set two feet farther west than where it stands today. There is ample evidence that in the original scheme it was the intention to have the west cross-wall and the western wall respectively one and two feet farther west than they were built.[1] At the north the great North Door was to stand on the axis of the hall, directly opposite to the stairway at the south. Along the east and west walls of the hall benches were to run; the ends of these, with the North Door, would practically fill the whole north wall. On the outside the North Door determined the axis of the wide North Porch. This was designed to cover and enclose the crypt with the god-wrought holes in the rock, to which there was to be an underground access from the interior of the building. The crypt fixed approximately the east line of the porch, and symmetry with this, about the door, brought the west line of the porch beyond the west wall of the building proper, so that it overlapped the north wall of the enclosure to the west. Aesthetically the result is unfortunate, but practically it permitted a door,—though one only about one metre wide, with the west wall in its originally intended position,—from the North Porch into the enclosure. Possibly there was an ancient entrance at this point which it was desired to perpetuate.

At the south, I believe it to have been the original intention to run the stairs straight up into the Porch of the Maidens, without any turn or landing, and to place the entrance, or rather the exit from the porch, in the middle of the south side, directly opposite the head of the stairs, and on axis with the hall below (Fig. 8, A). My chief reason for believing this is that the present arrangement is incredibly awkward (Fig. 8, B). The stairs are turned at right angles in as clumsy a way as could well be imagined, and in a way that would be distinctly dangerous to anyone descending them. The upper run of steps is only two-thirds as wide as the lower run, and at the head, instead of coming opposite the exit from the porch, the top step is partly masked by an anta, only 90 cm. away, which projects for a quarter of the width of the stair. Had the porch been built where originally intended, this anta would have come one Attic foot, —0.327 m.,—closer still (Fig. 8, C). But with the porch in the intended position the stairs could have been run straight for their full

[1] This evidence, which to me is entirely convincing, will be fully presented by Mr. Hill in the American School's publication of the Erechtheum, now in press, and consequently I shall not discuss it here, further than to mention two points which Mr. Hill brings out: first,—the sill of the North Door, laid before the west cross-wall or the west wall had been built, shows well-marked *anathyroses* for two bench ends, and thereby locates the intended positions of the north-south walls against which they were to lie; second,—the coffering of the ceiling of the Porch of the Maidens indicates that the porch was originally intended to be one foot wider, from east to west, than it was actually built.

width,—1.314 m.,—and would have landed about one and a quarter metres back from the opening in the centre of the south wall. The extra foot, if distributed equally among the three bays between the

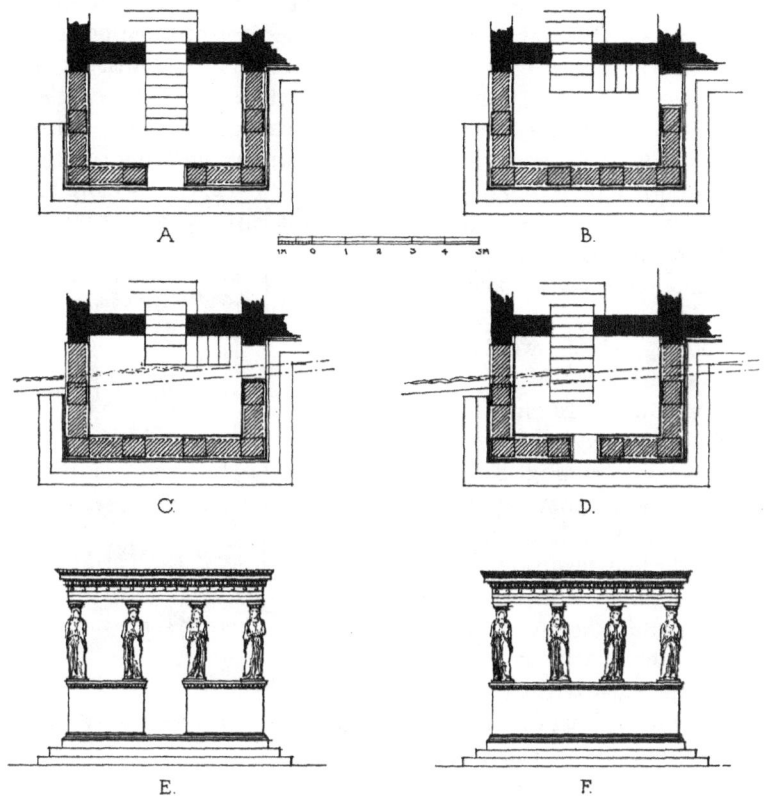

FIGURE 8. PORCH OF THE MAIDENS.

maidens, would have given an opening about 1.10 m. wide; or if the centre opening had been made wider than the side ones, it could have been of the full width of the stairs (Fig. 8, A and E).[1] But the actual

[1] There are a series of roundels or uncut rosettes on the top band of the architrave, above the caryatids. One of these comes directly above the axis of each of the two more central capitals of the façade (Fig. 8, F). Between these there are four other roundels, all spaced 0.34 m. on centres. At the corners of the porch the roundels do not come over the axes of the capitals, but are moved outward, as are the corner triglyphs of a Doric frieze, so that they are 0.36 m. distant, on centres, from their neighbors. Now if one more foot were added to the width of the porch, the increment (0.327 m.) might be divided among the fifteen interspaces of the roundels, increasing each by two centimetres, or an extra roundel unit might be introduced, in which case each axial distance would be decreased one millimetre. With the latter arrangement it is evident that the extra unit could not be distributed equally among the three bays, if a roundel is to come above the axis of the inner capitals, but would have to be added integrally to the width of the central bay, while the side bays would be diminished five millimetres each. This would

building of the Erechtheum was begun, apparently, at the east jamb of the South Door,[1] and the foundations were continued east from there along the south side, then across the east end, and the whole lower part of the north side was laid, at least up to and including the sill of the North Door, before it was decided to shift the position of the west wall and the Porch of the Maidens. The South Door, at the foot of the stairs, therefore, had to remain stationary while the axis of the porch was moved a foot and a half to the west. This, of course, made it necessary to change the stairway, in order to prevent it from debouching directly behind one of the Caryatids (Fig. 8, D). The stairs were naturally turned to the east, as only in that direction was there the necessary room for the run. But the heavy Kara stone foundations of the Hecatompedon, which would have been surmounted if the stairs had continued straight (Fig. 9), restricted the width of the platform at the turn (Fig. 8, C), and prevented the upper run of steps from being as wide as the lower one. For the resultant unsatisfactory arrangement the architect should, therefore, not be blamed, since it was clearly a makeshift dictated by circumstances beyond his control.

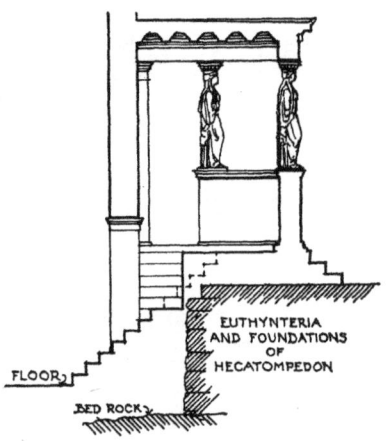

FIGURE 9. SECTION ON LINE OF EAST JAMB OF SOUTH DOOR

The function of the porch is evident: its existence was required by the existence of the stairs, to keep rain from flooding the lower hall. If the area occupied by the hall was unroofed, prior to the Periclean building, there would, of course, have been no necessity for roofing any preceding stairs, nor for covering their head with a porch. I think it probable, therefore, that the Porch of the Maidens, certainly the most famous single feature of the Erechtheum, is one of the very few which is not the successor of a similar construction on the same site.[2]

---

make the central bay 2.061 m. between the axes of the capitals, 1.302 m. in the clear between the plinths on which the caryatids stand, and four centimetres more between the jambs of an opening in the podium below. The width of the south door of the Erechtheum, at the point where the steps pass through, is 1.314 m.; so that the steps would be about three centimetres narrower than the opening in the podium.

[1] See Erechtheum Papers I, *A.J.A.* XXVIII, p. 14, and fig. 11.
[2] In the Acropolis Museum at Athens are a considerable number of archaic female marble figures, which, having been damaged when the Persians burned the Acropolis, were respectfully buried not far to the north-west of the Erechtheum, prob-

The width of the porch, from east to west, was obviously determined by the width of the hall within, and changed when the latter was changed. The natural proportion of two bays of depth to three of width, as in the North Porch, determined its extent from north to south.

The position of the north wall of the Erechtheum may have been affected by some arrangement of the "west cella" *temenos*, of which we have no material remains. If it had been built as close as possible against the terrace wall of the Cimonian "east cella" *temenos*, it would have been a metre and a half south of its actual position. This would have left the terrace walk, somewhat reduced in width, outside to the north, flanking the "theatral area," and so far as the eastern section is concerned, would have exactly reproduced the previous arrangement. But the "west cella" *temenos* was on the same level as the terrace walk, and may very well have included the western extension of the latter within its sacred area. In that case the new wall would necessarily have been placed at the north line of the terrace walk, so as not to cut off the latter from the rest of the "west cella" *temenos*.

At the east end of the building, it was decided to continue the grade level in front of the Hecatompedon clear to the north wall of the Acropolis. Why this was decided I do not know, nor can I guess where the quantity of earth necessary for the fill was found. It must have been a laborious and expensive undertaking. But as a result

---

ably at the time of the Cimonian reconstruction. (See Cavvadias und Kawerau, *op. cit.*, pp. 23–30, and figs. 1, 2.) These figures are undoubtedly votive offerings which were set up, on high columnar pedestals, during the sixth and early fifth centuries, somewhere in the vicinity of the shrine of Athena Polias. The position which seems to me to have been preëminently suitable for such statues is the stylobate of the north peristyle of the Hecatompedon, particularly in the eastern section. For there could have been no direct circulation between the columns into the "east cella" *temenos*, which lay a metre below the stylobate, while to the "west cella" *temenos* there was a sheer drop of two and a half metres. Now the cults and rites of Athens survived the fire, and votive female statues, changing in style with the times though probably always slightly archaistic, continued doubtless to be dedicated by priestesses and *Arrephoroi*. Pausanias mentions (Bk. I, 27, 4) a statue of the aged priestess Lysimache, "near the temple of Athena." It is likely that the foundations of the Pisistratid colonnade, which continued as a terrace wall, were adorned with new "*korai*" on high pedestals, some of them half a century old, at the time the new Erechtheum was begun. It seems probable to me that when the architect was called on to design a porch to cover the head of the little semi-private south stairway, which should not at all compete with the colonnaded porticoes at the north and east, it was the adjacent row of votive marble females which suggested to him the idea of supporting his porch roof on caryatids instead of upon columns. The caryatid although a well-established motif in Ionic architecture, as in the treasuries at Delphi, had hitherto been used only for supports between *antae*, and never, so far as we know, had an open porch, —not only prostyle, but with open supports on the sides,—been carried entirely on female heads. I do not believe that the maidens of the porch (refered to simply as *korai* in the building inscription) had any especial significance, either religious or mythological, but rather that they were supposed to count merely as six more votive statues, which should dominate and blend with the rows of their sisters stretching to east and west, and thus render the little porch at once harmonious with its surroundings, and inconspicuous.

of this decision, twelve steps were required to mount from the "theatral area" up to the new level at the east, where six had served in the Cimonian arrangement. To keep such a large flight within reasonable dimensions the east terrace walk was eliminated, and with great architectural cleverness the steps were united to the podium of the East Portico, against which they abutted. The arrangement— not to go into its details—required that the bottom of the stairs should commence just to the west of the inner line of the east wall of the Erechtheum, and brought the top at about the line of the stylobate of the east portico. This being the case, if the bottom of the stairs had been set at the line of the bottom of the Cimonian steps, then the new "east cella" *temenos* would have been extended to the east by two-thirds of its original size. On the other hand, had the earlier east line of the *temenos* been maintained, then the "theatral area" would have been encroached upon by the new stairs, to the extent of nearly four metres. The line adopted is a compromise, the east cella being enlarged by one metre, and the "theatral area" decreased by three. And by extending the "theatral area" at the west, up to the new North Porch, the lost three metres were gained again.

The terrace walk at the south and east sides of the "theatral area" being thus eliminated from the plan, it would have presented an awkward, unbalanced appearance to leave the section along the north side. So it, too, was removed, and the new pavement of the "theatral area" was extended clear to the north wall of the Acropolis. Evidence of this is to be found in the damaged drums of the Parthenon, which were used as foundations for the wall at this point. The second drum to the east of the reëntrant angle in the wall has a shallow circular cutting in its upper surface, as if to receive the base of a small stone shaft. The next drum to the east is cut down all the way across its top, for a depth of 20–25 cm., leaving, along the base of the poros wall, a band a little under 20 cm. wide, at the original level. A small continuation of this cutting appears on the column drum previously mentioned. The rectangular cut in the second and third drums shows clearly in the photograph, (*A.J.A.* XXVIII, p. 148, fig. 4.) but the circular cut is barely visible. Evidently a rectangular base, slightly longer than the diameter of a column drum, stood here against the Acropolis wall. The cuttings for the rectangular and circular bases are both well made, the workmanship is certainly Greek or very good Roman. So it is evident that the north terrace of the "theatral area" was removed before the beginning of our era. And as there is no indication of any alteration in the Erechtheum or its surroundings between the time of Cimon and that of Augustus, save that at the time of the classic Periclean building,—at which time it is certain that the "theatral area" was paved with marble, and the steps on the east side built,—I can see no reason to doubt that the little terrace against the north wall was removed then. The lower part of the wall, which was previously hidden by the terrace, is built of rough unsightly re-used poros blocks, and must have been covered up again by a veneer, probably of marble slabs, and as the cutting in the third column drum indicates, less than 0.20 m. thick.

The Periclean "theatral area" was, then, approximately the same in length from east to west as its forerunner, though somewhat shifted to the west. Its width was increased by 2.00–3.50 m. along the northern side, and the wide and high new steps on the east increased the space available for a standing audience by about 50 per cent beyond that of the Cimonian arrangement. The North Porch also provided considerable standing room for spectators, though whether this was a gain or not is uncertain, since we do not know what preceded it in that location. The only loss to offset these gains was the terrace walk, which obviously was not in any way a sacred area. The windows in the north wall, of course, became useless after the removal of the north terrace walk; wherefore we may presume that though they are today the sole surviving windows, they probably were only two of many in the circuit of the Acropolis, and had no particular religious or other significance.

The position of the south wall of the Erechtheum may have been determined by the desire to keep the "east cella" *temenos* of the same width as in the post-Persian revision; or it may have been determined by something in the "west cella" *temenos* of which we now know nothing; or if the foundations of the Hecatompedon were not trimmed back to the line Z (Fig. 1), it may be that a desire to carry the new south wall on entirely new foundations, clear to bed rock, caused the south face of the wall to be set just north of the northernmost point of the Hecatompedon. I rather doubt this latter reason, however, as I think it much more probable that the south line of the Cimonian "east cella" *temenos* was Z rather than Y (Fig. 1), and I do not believe that the Periclean builders would have hesitated to support a wall partly on old foundations and partly on new.

The east cross-wall within the Erechtheum was, of course, fixed by the west terrace-wall of the "east cella" *temenos*. Its western face seems to have lain one Attic foot west of that of the older wall, but where it joins the north and south walls of the Erechtheum the trace is two feet wide,—the normal width for Erechtheum walls. Apparently a full new wall was not built against the terrace wall for fear of encroaching unduly upon the "west cella" *temenos*, but a sturdy marble veneer, one foot thick,—which seems, incidentally, not to have required any new foundations, since there are no cuttings in the Acropolis rock,—was applied to the poros wall, which, in turn, had been built upon the base of, and in part against, the heavy

Mycaenean wall. Mr. Stevens has discovered[1] that while the stones of the east cross-wall do not tongue into the north and south walls in their lower parts, yet above the floor level of the eastern cella they do so. In the lower parts L-shaped stones, one arm of which was part of the regular ashlar of the north and south walls, projected perhaps one and three feet alternately, or perhaps more or less, to meet the veneer stones of the cross-wall. The projecting parts have now all been chiseled off. Probably the north and south walls were built to a considerable height before the cross-wall was veneered or the "east cella" *temenos* disturbed by raising its floor to its classic level: but when this had been done and the cross-wall veneered, the upper parts of the north and south and cross-walls were probably built simultaneously, all of blocks two feet thick, with alternate courses of the cross-wall tonguing into those at its ends. The lower construction with L blocks, which are expensive in material and workmanship, is quite abnormal, and supports the belief that in its lower part the cross-wall had not the normal thickness of two feet, as it had above. It is certainly not ideal construction to carry a two-foot marble wall half on an old poros wall and half on a new marble one-foot facing, but with the blocks tied each to the others with iron clamps and dowels, as was customary in Greek work, and with the foundations going to bed rock, the wall would actually be amply strong. And that the architect of the Erechtheum would not have hesitated to build in this manner is evident, for, in the south wall of the building, the exterior base course and the orthostates above it were backed on the inside for their full length by wall courses, one of which,—that against the base course,—is only one and a third feet thick, while the two above are only one foot thick. The upper two courses have now all fallen away, probably as the result of the fire which badly calcined the interior of the building, but the wall apparently still stood. The construction here is, in principle, identical with that suggested for the east cross-wall.

I have made no attempt in this paper to give a full explanation of how the Erechtheum was designed, and many factors now unknown undoubtedly had influence upon the plan. The suggestion of Dr. Doerpfeld, that originally the architect conceived a building which should be symmetrical about the axis of the North Porch and the hall leading therefrom to the Porch of the Maidens, with a west wing enclosing the Pandroseum to balance the present eastern part, seems to me quite within the possibilities. The fact that the distance from the axis to the western end of the Pandroseum is practically the same as that to the eastern wall of the Erechtheum lends strength to this hypothesis, and the latter wall may well have been built to the east

---

[1] Detailed description with drawings of the significant stones will appear in the American School's publication of the Erechtheum.

of its Cimonian predecessor in order to balance the westward extent of the Pandroseum. But while the building may have been designed to be symmetrical from without, it could never have been so in the arrangement of the rooms within. For, as we shall see in a later paper, the area which would have formed the western wing was divided lengthwise from east to west, with the southern part on a higher level than the northern; while that of the eastern wing,— which was actually built,—was divided transversely from north to south, with the eastern part on a higher level than the western. And it seems certain to me that by the time the west wall of the classic structure was begun, all idea of a symmetrical building was definitely abandoned. In any case, the fifth-century architect was at no time free to plan a structure wholly new, the form of which was subject only to his judgment; his problem was rather how to house a congeries of old and very sacred *temene*, whose positions might not be changed nor areas at all reduced. So while there is a strong suggestion that a symmetrical scheme was originally designed, yet it is also quite possible that the strange irregularities of the existing building may be accounted for by irregularities in what was there before, and do not need the hypothesis of any change in plan to make them rational.

LEICESTER B. HOLLAND

PHILADELPHIA

www.ingramcontent.com/pod-product-compliance
Lightning Source LLC
Chambersburg PA
CBHW020809160426
43192CB00006B/494